GRAND PRIX YEAR 01/02
HAZLETON PUBLISHING

PUBLISHER
RICHARD POULTER

EDITOR
SIMON ARRON

WRITTEN BY
SIMON ARRON & TONY DODGINS

ART EDITOR
RYAN BAPTISTE

RESULTS & DATA
DAVID HAYHOE

PRODUCTION MANAGER
STEVEN PALMER

PUBLISHING DEVELOPMENT MANAGER
SIMON SANDERSON

SALES PROMOTION
ANNALISA ZANELLA

PHOTOGRAPHY
LAT PHOTOGRAPHIC & MARTYN ELFORD

GRAPHICS
RUSSELL LEWIS

ALL RESULTS AND DATA
© FIA 2001

GRAND PRIX YEAR

is published by
Hazleton Publishing Ltd.
3 Richmond Hill
Richmond, Surrey
TW10 6RE, England

**Colour reproduction and Printing by
The 5 Core Group Ltd, Newbury**

© Hazleton Publishing Ltd. 2001,
a part of the Profile Media Group PLC

ISBN: 1 903135 21 4

FEATURES

www.hazletonpublishing.com

DISTRIBUTORS

UNITED KINGDOM
Haynes Publishing
Sparkford
Nr Yeovil
Somerset
BA22 7JJ
Tel: 01963 440635
Fax: 01963 440001

NORTH AMERICA
Motorbooks International
PO Box 1
729 Prospect Ave.
Osceola
Wisconsin 54020, USA
Tel: (1) 715 294 3345
Fax: (1) 715 294 4448

REST OF THE WORLD
Menoshire Ltd
Unit 13
Wadsworth Road
Perivale
Middlesex UB6 7LQ
Tel: 020 8566 7344
Fax: 020 8991 2439

2001 FIA FORMULA ONE WORLD CHAMPIONSHIP

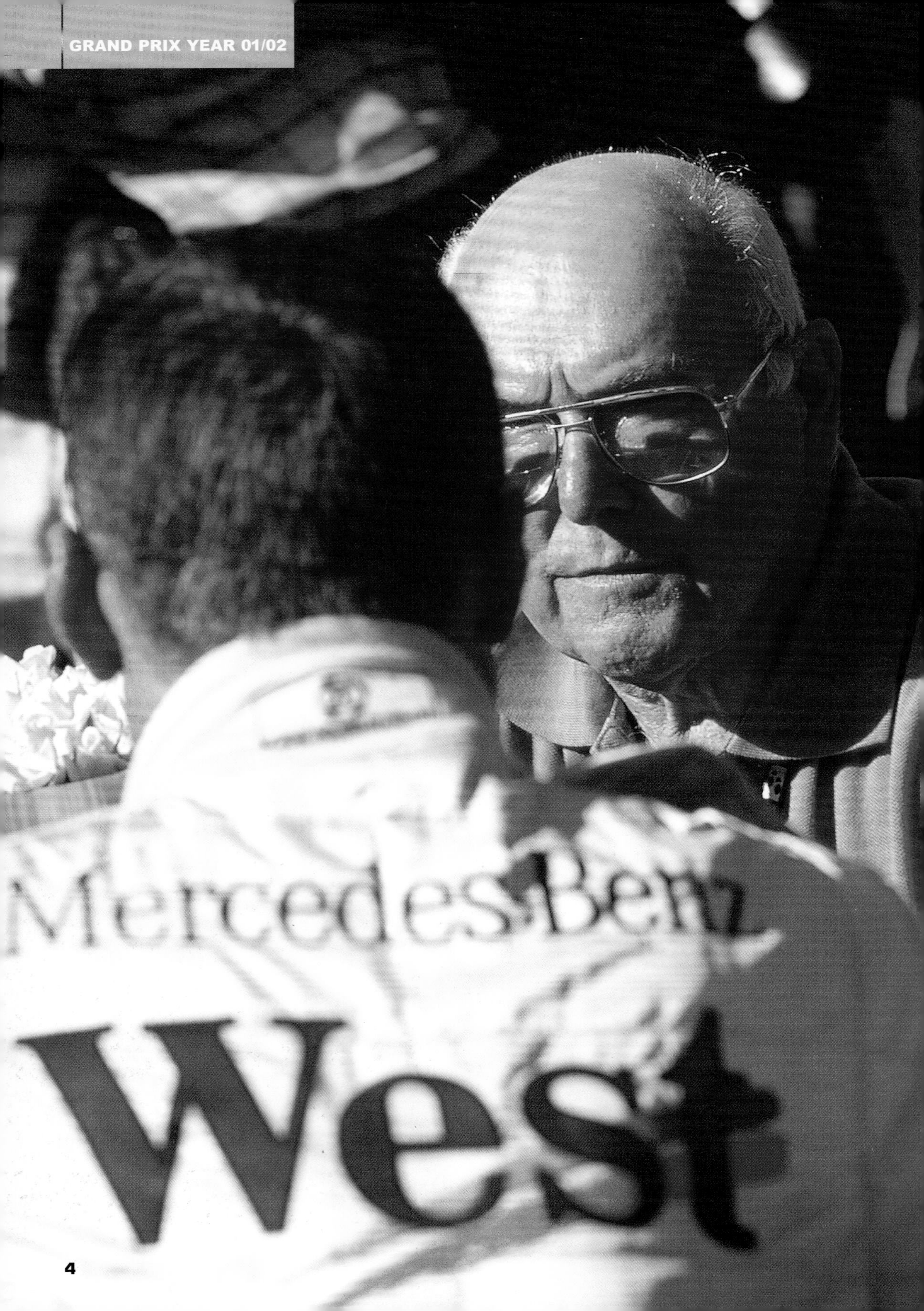
Mercedes-Benz
West

FOREWORD BY MURRAY WALKER

FERRARI MIGHT HAVE WAITED 21 YEARS FOR A WORLD championship to come along, but having finally rediscovered the knack in 2000, the legendary Italian team shows no sign of losing its grip.

This has been some season for Michael Schumacher and Ferrari. The gifted German wrapped up his fourth world title with several races to spare – and at Spa he broke Alain Prost's all-time record of 51 grand prix wins. Fitting that he should do it on the 10th anniversary of his F1 baptism, too.

While I can't see Schuey being knocked off that particular perch, however, I think he'll need to fight harder than ever in future to build on his imposing record.

Michael's younger brother Ralf is getting better all the time – as is his BMW-Williams team. Juan Pablo Montoya proved to be every bit as spectacular as we had hoped and is clearly going to be a thorn in the side of both Schumachers. McLaren had a subdued campaign by its own standards in 2001 and won't take that lying down. And while Ron Dennis's men might be losing the services of Mika Hakkinen, for now at least, his replacement Kimi Raikkonen looks to be just as exciting a prospect as Montoya. There are signs that Renault is beginning to make giant steps in the right direction, too, so there could be more potential race winners on the grid in 2002 than we have seen for some time. And guess who won't be there to see it...

Actually that's not quite true. I might be stepping down from the commentary box after 52 years, but I have been inundated with offers to stay in F1 and I'm going to take time mulling them over.

One thing's for sure, I'm not going to walk away from the sport altogether. I love it too much – and you can read some of the reasons why here in *Grand Prix Year*, a colourful, irreverent review of another high-octane campaign. I know I'll enjoy what follows and hope you will too.

THE CLASS OF

SCUDERIA FERRARI-MARLBORO
FERRARI F2001-FERRARI V10

IN A NUTSHELL Defending the drivers' title for the first time since 1980. Stable, effective technical team headed by Ross Brawn, the shrewdest race tactician in the business (he went to Manchester Grammar School, just like England test opener Michael Atherton; no prizes for guessing which of them had the best summer)

DRIVERS MICHAEL SCHUMACHER (D) – best in the world, both in his own mind and by general consensus. Has three world titles to prove it. Sorry, make that four

RUBENS BARRICHELLO (BR) – genuinely decent bloke, but persistently a tenth or seven slower than his team-mate. Much better than the average BSM graduate, then, but no Schuey

TEST DRIVER LUCA BADOER (I) – gets paid loads to hang around the team's Fiorano test track, despite not being a top-liner. Nice work if you can get it

WEST McLAREN-MERCEDES
McLAREN MP4-16-MERCEDES V10

West McLaren Mercedes

IN A NUTSHELL Driver line-up unchanged for the sixth straight season – a world and Olympic record. Relying on a modified version of the previous year's effective V10, unlike main rivals Ferrari and Williams who invested in newer technology. On the verge of an unsettling personnel crisis because Jaguar boss Bobby Rahal wanted to pinch star technical director Adrian Newey (the American failed, however, and was soon axed)

DRIVERS MIKA HAKKINEN (FIN) – double world champion whose competitive edge might just have been dulled by pre-season birth of son Hugo. Taking a break from F1 in 2002, although we could swear he began doing that several months ago

DAVID COULTHARD (GB) – having been all but ignored by the British tabloid media for years, because he generally leads a settled life, he moved from the back pages to the front just before the start of the season thanks to a string of high-profile dalliances (plus an incident involving some bubble bath and a girl called Ruth)

TEST DRIVERS ALEXANDER WURZ (A) – tall Benetton reject. When not driving racing cars, likes paragliding off the tallest Alps he can find. **DARREN TURNER (GB)** – drives for Mercedes in the German-based DTM touring car series (which, we feel duty-bound to point out, is completely crap, despite what Merc would have you believe). Fills in for McLaren as and when

...OR A ROUGH GUIDE TO WHO AND WHAT LURKS IN THOSE OPULENT MOTORHOMES BEYOND THE ELECTRONICALLY-CONTROLLED PADDOCK GATES THAT DENY ACCESS TO ALL BUT THE PRIVILEGED FEW (AND GASTON MAZZACANE, SOMETIMES)

BMW WILLIAMSF1
WILLIAMS FW23-BMW V10

BMW.WilliamsF1 Team

IN A NUTSHELL Team trying to claw its way back to the kind of success it enjoyed in the Nineties with Nigel Mansell, Alain Prost, Damon Hill and Jacques Villeneuve. BMW is good at feigning modesty about its prospects – but is even better at making engines

DRIVERS RALF SCHUMACHER (D) – younger brother of you-know-who and improving by the lap. Most drivers choose to live in Monaco, but he prefers Austria. Science is powerless to explain that one

JUAN PABLO MONTOYA (CO) – firebrand behind the wheel, very bloody funny to talk to. More hype than Big Brother. Unlike the latter, however, he's worth the fuss

TEST DRIVER MARC GENÉ (E) – shall I race a Minardi or test a Williams? Not too tough a choice, frankly

MILD SEVEN BENETTON RENAULT SPORT
BENETTON B201-RENAULT V10

Benetton Formula 1 RACING TEAM

IN A NUTSHELL First year of partnership with former F1 colossus Renault, which takes full control from 2002. Everyone knows the engine will work eventually. Worrying thing is that some believe this might not be until halfway through next season...

DRIVERS GIANCARLO FISICHELLA (I) – fast, especially in Montreal and Monte Carlo, but with questionable technical ability. Says "very happy" a lot, apart from when he isn't (which would quite often be the case in 2001)

JENSON BUTTON (GB) – naturally quick, as he proved in a gilt-edged 2000 Williams-BMW, but desperately short of experience when it comes to sorting out all-new packages

TEST DRIVER MARK WEBBER (AUS) – level-headed quote machine. Fitter than the regular racers. Some believe he is technically more gifted and at least as fast

LUCKY STRIKE REYNARD BAR RACING HONDA
BAR 003-HONDA V10

IN A NUTSHELL Promised to win its maiden race in 1999, but we're still waiting. Partner Honda has a peerless reputation as an F1 engine builder, but it reappeared on the scene at the same time as BMW in 2000 and has been slower to make progress

DRIVERS JACQUES VILLENEUVE (CDN) – winning the world title with Williams in 1997 must feel like a long time ago. The only man in the field with a part-share in a four-storey restaurant in Montreal

OLIVIER PANIS (F) – back in the frontline after a season testing for McLaren (which offered him a bigger salary than BAR in an effort to persuade him not to move). But he's a racer

TEST DRIVERS About half the world's competition licence holders... **DARREN MANNING (GB)**, **TAKUMA SATO (J)**, **ANTHONY DAVIDSON (GB)** and **PATRICK LEMARIÉ (F)**. Three of them have real potential; Lemarié is Villeneuve's childhood buddy

BENSON & HEDGES JORDAN-HONDA
JORDAN EJ11-HONDA V10

IN A NUTSHELL First season as an official Honda partner after a long, mostly fruitful association with its offshoot Mugen. The 10th anniversary of the team's F1 baptism, when Eddie Jordan managed to complete an F1 season for about the price of a round in a city-centre pub

DRIVERS HEINZ-HARALD FRENTZEN (D) – an outside contender for world championship honours just a couple of seasons ago, but sacked in July 2001 after a string of results that were poor, but hardly a red card offence

JARNO TRULLI (I) – very fast and a great qualifier, but with an inexplicable tendency to nod off during races

RICARDO ZONTA (BR) – dumped by BAR so took job as Jordan tester. Given a couple of chances to revive his career as sub for Frentzen, but didn't impress and returned to the subs' bench with rather more haste than he had driven

JEAN ALESI (F) – won the 1989 FIA F3000 title with Jordan. Recalled in August, at the age of 37, to take over from sacked Frentzen and tugging Zonta

TEST DRIVER ZONTA (see above)

ORANGE ARROWS-ASIATECH
ARROWS A22-ASIATECH V10

IN A NUTSHELL First – and only – season with the Asiatech V10, a rebadged version of the Peugeot engine that used to go wrong a lot when fitted to a Prost

DRIVERS JOS VERSTAPPEN (NL) – feisty Dutchman, but you'd think after eight seasons that his compatriots would leave their "Jos the Boss" flags at home. He isn't

ENRIQUE BERNOLDI (BR) – Brazilian rookie. Very experienced at suffering car breakages while running at – or near – the front in FIA F3000 races

TEST DRIVER JOHNNY HERBERT (GB) – amusing old bloke given something to do after his plans to land a Champ Car deal in the United States fell flat

RED BULL SAUBER PETRONAS
SAUBER C20-PETRONAS V10

IN A NUTSHELL The arrival of a youthful and dynamic driver line-up jolts slumbering Swiss team into life for just about the first time since its F1 debut in 1993

DRIVERS NICK HEIDFELD (D) – gifted, but ignorantly dismissed by many who should know better after he struggled with Prost the previous season. Even Schuey would have been crap in a 2000 Prost

KIMI RAIKKONEN (FIN) – extraordinary newcomer. Graduating from Formula Renault to F1 is a leap that would have taxed Carl Lewis. But apparently possible. The big guns soon tried to tempt him away with bags of sweets and offers of a subscription to the Beano (well, the Finnish Beano). By September, McLaren had him nailed

TEST DRIVER What do you need one of those for when your boundlessly energetic regular racers have a combined age of about 14?

JAGUAR RACING
JAGUAR R2-FORD COSWORTH V10

IN A NUTSHELL Second season in F1 – and the first under management of wily (or wily but sacked, as things turned out) American Bobby Rahal and triple world champion Niki Lauda. Back-to-basics engineering approach promised more in the way of reliability than speed, however

DRIVERS EDDIE IRVINE (GB) – criticised for his passion for boats, planes and women. Er, why? Does a bloody good job during most race weekends, so leave him alone

LUCIANO BURTI (BR) – former test driver struggled in the opening few races and was swiftly packed off to Prost

PEDRO DE LA ROSA (E) – experienced and capable, he was nicked from Prost as tester at the start of the season, then promoted at Burti's expense

TEST DRIVER TOMAS SCHECKTER (ZA) – well, he was until he picked up a fine for kerb-crawling in Northampton. Lauda said he didn't mind what Irvine got up to in-between races; that didn't apply to junior members of staff, obviously

EUROPEAN MINARDI F1
MINARDI PS01-EUROPEAN V10

IN A NUTSHELL Ailing Italian team rescued five minutes before the start of the season by Aussie racing nut Paul Stoddart, who made his fortune selling aviation spares. Neat chassis – but team handicapped by Ford-based V10 that's not much newer than the Model T

DRIVERS FERNANDO ALONSO (E) – Formula Nissan champion at 17, FIA F3000 front-runner at 18, F1 driver at 19. Exceptional potential

TARSO MARQUES (BR) – not very good in a Minardi in 1996 or 1997

ALEX YOONG (MAL) – first Malaysian to drive an F1 car; called up because Marques proved not to be very good in a Minardi in 2001, either

TEST DRIVERS Just about everybody who hasn't been mentioned so far, but principally **ANDREA PICCINI (I), CHRISTIJAN ALBERS (NL)** and **DAVID SAELENS (B)**

PROST-ACER
PROST AP04-ACER V10

IN A NUTSHELL Not quite the disaster movie on wheels it was in 2000, thanks mainly to the arrival of year-old, bombproof Ferrari engines (rebadged as Acers for commercial reasons)
DRIVERS JEAN ALESI (F) – most experienced man in the field and the best finisher in the business. Gets very excited about scoring points in a Prost and tends to throw his helmet into the crowd. With an Indian summer in sight, he cleared off to Jordan before the end of the season
GASTON MAZZACANE (ARG) – great at bringing sponsorship, not terribly good at driving. Pitched after four races, which was about four too many
LUCIANO BURTI (BR) – did much better in a Prost than he did in a Jaguar. Then came Spa
HEINZ-HARALD FRENTZEN (D) – said he was pleased to be joining Prost after Jordan sacked him. Bit like saying you were looking forward to joining Shrewsbury Town after several seasons with Manchester United
TOMAS ENGE (CZ) – there were rumours about Prost bouncing cheques; by Monza the team also had a bouncing Czech
TEST DRIVERS PEDRO DE LA ROSA (E) – for about five minutes, until Jaguar pinched him
STÉPHANE SARRAZIN (F) – quick, but underused
JONATHAN COCHET (F) – French F3 champ in 2000, but virtually penniless (a bit like Prost)

PANASONIC TOYOTA
TOYOTA TF 101-TOYOTA V10

IN A NUTSHELL Testing only this year. Coming to F1 in 2002 and winding up various teams by nicking key staff (particularly Minardi, whose designer Gustav Brunner was swiped early on)
DRIVERS ALLAN McNISH (GB) – poised to be the Jenson Button of the previous generation, but unfairly cast aside when the world appeared to be at his feet as a 20-year-old. If he lines up on the grid in Australia next season he'll be 32. Potentially a great comeback story – and it would be thoroughly deserved. He is set to make his F1 debut after 1988 team-mate Mika Hakkinen has retired (sorry, taken a break from F1)
MIKA SALO (FIN) – F1 veteran who was one of McNish's rivals in the 1989 British F3 Championship. Since then, he's started 93 more grands prix than Allan

A MATTER OF FACTS

A TOTAL OF 26 DRIVERS STARTED AT LEAST ONE WORLD CHAMPIONSHIP GRAND PRIX THIS YEAR – AND MOST ARE TOO YOUNG TO HAVE EXPERIENCED THE MOST IMPORTANT THINGS IN LIFE (THE BEATLES, ESSO'S 1970 WORLD CUP COIN COLLECTION, THE RALEIGH CHOPPER). STILL, AT LEAST _THUNDERBIRDS_ IS NOW BEING REPEATED FOR THEIR BENEFIT

DRIVER	BORN	FIRST GRAND PRIX
Jean Alesi	Jun 11 1964	France 1989, Tyrrell
Fernando Alonso	Jul 29 1981	Australia 2001, Minardi
Rubens Barrichello	May 23 1972	South Africa 1993, Jordan
Enrique Bernoldi	Oct 19 1978	Australia 2001, Arrows
Luciano Burti	Mar 5 1973	Austria 2000, Jaguar
Jenson Button	Jan 18 1980	Australia 2000, Williams
David Coulthard	Mar 27 1971	Spain 1994, Williams
Pedro de la Rosa	Feb 24 1971	Australia 1999, Arrows
Tomas Enge	Sep 11 1976	Italy 2001, Prost
Giancarlo Fisichella	Jan 14 1973	Australia 1996, Minardi
Heinz-Harald Frentzen	May 18 1967	Brazil 1994, Sauber
Mika Hakkinen	Sep 28 1968	United States 1991, Lotus
Nick Heidfeld	May 10 1977	Australia 2000, Prost
Eddie Irvine	Nov 10 1965	Japan 1993, Jordan
Tarso Marques	Jan 19 1976	Brazil 1996, Minardi
Gaston Mazzacane	May 8 1975	Australia 2000, Minardi
Juan Pablo Montoya	Sep 20 1975	Australia 2001, Williams
Olivier Panis	Sep 2 1966	Brazil 1994, Ligier
Kimi Raikkonen	Oct 17 1979	Australia 2001, Sauber
Michael Schumacher	Jan 3 1969	Spa 1991, Jordan
Ralf Schumacher	Jun 20 1975	Australia 1997, Jordan
Jarno Trulli	Jul 13 1974	Australia 1997, Minardi
Jos Verstappen	Mar 4 1972	Brazil 1994, Benetton
Jacques Villeneuve	Apr 9 1971	Australia 1996, Williams
Alex Yoong	Jul 20 1976	Italy 2001, Minardi
Ricardo Zonta	Mar 23 1976	Australia 1999, BAR

* world and Olympic record; includes 78 scored in 1997, when he was stripped of second place for being a thug altho

TOTAL STARTS	WINS	POLES	POINTS SCORED
201	1	2	241
17	0	0	0
147	1	3	195
17	0	0	0
15	0	0	0
34	0	0	14
124	11	12	359
46	0	0	6
3	0	0	0
91	0	1	75
129	3	2	159
162	20	26	420
33	0	0	12
129	4	0	183
25	0	0	0
21	0	0	0
17	1	3	31
108	1	0	61
17	0	0	9
160	53	43	801*
83	3	1	135
78**	0	0	29
91	0	0	17
98	11	13	209
3	0	0	0
30	0	0	3

wins and points still count (got this bit wrong last season, sorry)   **only awake for about half of them

QANTAS AUSTRALIAN GRAND PRIX

TWO DAYS AFTER LANDING ON HIS HEAD IN A GRAVEL TRAP, MICHAEL SCHUMACHER GOT HIS WORLD TITLE DEFENCE OFF TO A SOLID START THANKS TO AN ALTOGETHER DIFFERENT KIND OF FLYING. BUT EVENTS ELSEWHERE ON THE TRACK MEANT THIS WAS NO TIME FOR CELEBRATION

HAKKED OFF: grumpy Mika strolls in (left) after McLaren inadvertently gave him a car with Morris Marina-style collapsible front suspension. Schuey was so far ahead by the end that he had time to conduct a rendition of Verdi's La Traviata (above) before his rivals crossed the line

DURING FRIDAY'S FREE PRACTICE SESSION PRIOR TO THE
Australian Grand Prix, Michael Schumacher brought gasps from
the audience when he pirouetted off the track, slammed sideways
into a gravel trap and launched his Ferrari into a series of rolls.

It appeared to be more of a fright, however, for those watching
than it did for the bloke strapped inside the scarlet missile. Schuey
calmly got out and assessed the wreck – but he had done less
damage to his car than he did to his rivals' morale when he
breezed to pole position 24 hours later. With the advent of a new
tyre war, brought on by Michelin's return to F1 to face hitherto
exclusive supplier Bridgestone, the German beat the previous
year's pole position time by a cavalier 3.7 seconds. And this was
despite new FIA regulations that were aimed at making cars slower.

The race was something of a stroll, too. Ferrari locked out the
front row and Schuey predictably eclipsed slow-starting team-
mate Rubens Barrichello as the pack filed through the first turn.
And that, basically, was that.

His serene progress was briefly interrupted from lap five,
because the Safety Car was deployed in the wake of the violent
accident between Jacques Villeneuve's BAR-Honda and the
Williams-BMW of the leader's younger brother Ralf. This, sadly,
had tragic consequences for one of the army of marshalling
volunteers whose presence is vital to the slick running of a grand
prix (see sidebar, opposite).

When the Safety Car pulled in again at the end of lap 15, Schuey
resumed where he had left off and paced himself no harder than
necessary to score his second successive win in Australia.

With Barrichello making a complete porridge of his start,

SCHUEY'S TRADITIONAL ARCH-RIVAL MIKA HAKKINEN LED THE CHASE UNTIL HIS McLAREN'S FRONT SUSPENSION BUCKLED ON THE 26TH LAP

Schuey's traditional arch-rival Mika Hakkinen led the chase until
his McLaren's front suspension buckled on the 26th lap and
pitched him into a tyre wall.

His team-mate David Coulthard ultimately took second. The
Scot, whose squeaky-clean image had been given something of a
pummelling by the British tabloids shortly before the season
kicked off (something to do with a bubble bath-related romp in a
London hotel with a girl other than his fiancée, who promptly
became his ex-fiancée when the story broke), was not at his
sharpest in qualifying, but he raced superbly and eventually
outfoxed Barrichello with a splendidly aggressive move.

Coulthard escaped unscathed after a brush with Heinz-Harald
Frentzen's Jordan on the run to the first corner at the start – but
that was nothing compared to what Barrichello got away with on
lap three, when he crudely shoved Frentzen into a gravel trap to
facilitate recovery from his sluggish start. The Brazilian went on to
take third and Frentzen drove spiritedly to haul his way back from
16th to fifth.

In his first drive for Sauber, Nick Heidfeld slotted between them
at the end. Unfairly ridiculed for his pointless campaign in a dog-

ROOM WITH A PHEW:
Coulthard (centre)
breathes in to avoid
hefty contact with
Frentzen at the start
(above), while Schuey
Jnr takes a wider, more
circumspect line. Right,
rescue crews clear up
after an outbreak of
Teutonic clumsiness
during practice

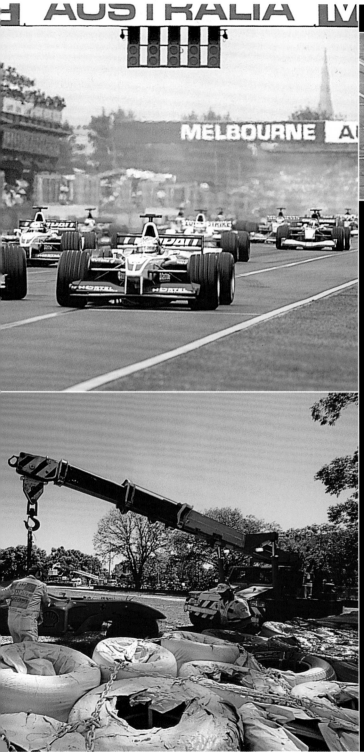

A HARSH TRUTH

Motor sport, in all its forms, can be dangerous. When you pay to watch, that message is there on the back of your admission ticket. And it is not just the drivers that are exposed to risk.

When Jacques Villeneuve's BAR cannoned into Ralf Schumacher's Williams on the fifth lap of the Australian GP (shortly after the picture above was taken), debris were flung far and wide. Carbon fibre shrapnel sprayed the crowd and a few spectators had to be treated for cuts and bruises.

Schumacher spun into the gravel, but Villeneuve's car was launched and slammed into the trackside safety fence before completing a dizzying series of rolls. During the car's erratic flight, a wheel penetrated a gap in the debris fencing and struck marshal Graham Beveridge in the chest. The 52-year-old died as a result. It marked the second time in five races that an unpaid official had perished while serving the sport (a loose wheel struck and killed fire marshal Paolo Ghislimberti during the 2000 Italian GP at Monza).

As a mark of respect, the drivers declined to spray champagne on the podium. Winner Michael Schumacher said: "We are all shocked and must look at what is possible from our side, to see what support we can give."

The gap in the fence was barely big enough to accommodate the wheel, but freakishly it struck at just the right angle to get through. It was a misfortune borne of improbability. No matter how much is done to make the sport safer, you can't legislate against every eventuality.

At Beveridge's funeral, his widow Karen said: "Graham died doing what he loved. He wasn't in the wrong place at the wrong time. He was in the right place at the wrong time."

ROOKIE IV, from left: Raikkonen, Montoya, Alonso and Bernoldi. Pass the Clearasil. . .

PARK SIDE OF THE MOON

IT WAS A PROMISING DAY FOR ROOKIE DRIVERS IN GENERAL

eared Prost during 2000, the former FIA F3000 champion knew he had proved a point after driving stylishly all weekend. "It's nice to be back in a good car," he said. His embryonic team-mate Kimi Raikkonen fared perhaps even better. The Formula Renault graduate barely put a wheel wrong and was rewarded with a championship point on his first F1 start, although both Saubers were only promoted when Olivier Panis's BAR, fourth on the road, was clobbered with a 30-second penalty for overtaking while yellow caution flags fluttered nearby.

It was a promising day for rookie drivers in general. Juan Pablo Montoya didn't get qualifying quite right (he was 11th, second-best Michelin runner but five places behind team-mate Schuey Jnr). Known for his fiery approach, the Colombian insisted his prime objective was to make the finish. "I have to gain experience," he said, "so I won't be doing anything rash."

The result? He was challenging Barrichello into the first corner, where he speared across the grass. Back on terra firma, he tipped Eddie Irvine's Jaguar into a spin at the third corner and then scorched through the field to vie for what would have been fourth place had his engine not exploded.

European Minardi newcomer Fernando Alonso, 19, also drove beautifully at the beginning of only his third season racing cars. He ran smoothly and tidily to finish 12th – not bad in a chassis that had barely covered any pre-race miles (especially as the Ford-based V10 within was almost as old, conceptually, as Fernando).

It was less positive for Arrows newcomer Enrique Bernoldi, who clipped a wall on only his second lap, while 2000 star Jenson Button discovered that life was not going be to quite so easy in a Benetton-Renault as it had been the previous year in a gilt-edged Williams-BMW. The young Englishman had a dreadful, character-building weekend in a car that generated little grip – and even less horsepower.

At least Button qualified on merit. Alonso's team-mate Tarso Marques failed to lap within the mandatory 107 per cent of the pole time, but was permitted to start because of "exceptional circumstances" (© the FIA). Other than the team recently having been bought by Paul Stoddart, an Australian businessman, nobody could fathom out what these were. ∎

It is late on Thursday evening at a tram stop close to the main entrance of Albert Park, home of the Australian Grand Prix since 1996.

At the far end of the platform, a man dressed all in red, with not very fetching scarlet wig, is struggling to stand up. Somewhat the worse for lager, he barks a few words at some locals. "Sorry, mate, not quite sure what you are trying to say," they mutter.

So he has another go: "I'shh, um, I'shh, hic, from Shermany!"

There are already about five German GPs (two in Germany, plus subsidiary beer festivals in Austria, Hungary and Belgium) – and here was a one-man attempt to establish a sixth.

Still, you couldn't blame him for having taken the trouble to travel. Getting blind-drunk in Melbourne has to be infinitely preferable to doing so at Hockenheim.

Melbourne first staged an Australian GP in 1953, 32 years before the nation hosted its maiden world championship event (in Adelaide). Then as now, the circuit wends its way around the picturesque Albert Park lake. It's a beautiful setting for a race – and the efficient local tram service means you aren't forced to put up with traffic jams.

The facilities have advanced a touch since the early days, although the same can't be said of some of the sideshows that were being promoted during the GP weekend. Deep Purple concert, anyone?

ACCESS RATING FOR BRITS ✴✴✴
A pain in the butt to get to – literally, if you fly economy class, because you are looking at more than 20 hours in the air. But it's worth the effort

STARTING GRID

Pos	Driver	Time
1	M Schumacher	1m26.892s
2	Barrichello	1m27.263s
3	Hakkinen	1m27.461s
11	Frentzen	1m27.658s
5	R Schumacher	1m27.719s
4	Coulthard	1m28.010s
12	Trulli	1m28.377s
10	Villeneuve	1m28.435s
9	Panis	1m28.518s
16	Heidfeld	1m28.615s
6	Montoya	1m28.738s
18	Irvine	1m28.965s
17	Raikkonen	1m28.993s
22	Alesi	1m29.893s
14	Verstappen	1m29.934s
8	Button	1m30.035s
7	Fisichella	1m30.209s
15	Bernoldi	1m30.520s
21	Alonso	1m30.657s
23	Mazzacane	1m30.798s
19	Burti	1m30.978s
20	Marques	1m33.228s

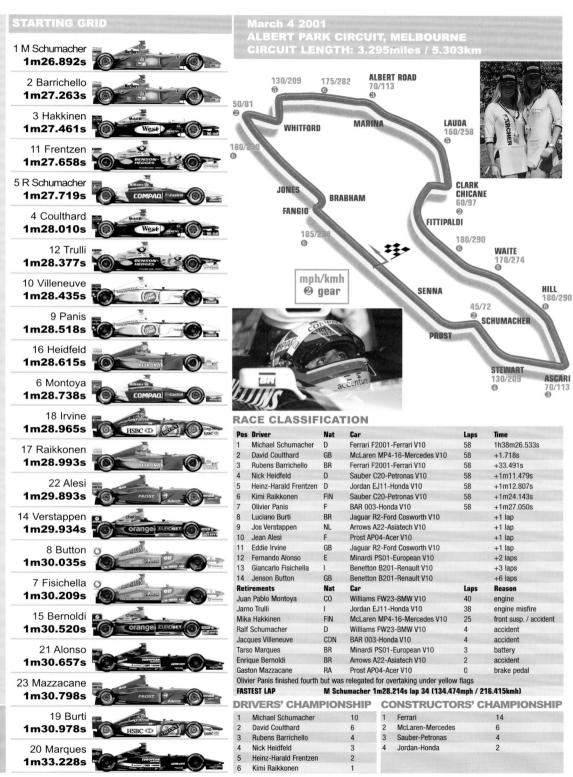

March 4 2001
ALBERT PARK CIRCUIT, MELBOURNE
CIRCUIT LENGTH: 3.295miles / 5.303km

130/209 ⑤
175/282 ⑥
ALBERT ROAD 70/113 ③
50/81 ②
WHITFORD
MARINA
LAUDA 160/258
180/290 ⑥
JONES
BRABHAM
CLARK CHICANE 60/97 ②
FANGIO
FITTIPALDI
185/298 ⑥
180/290
WAITE 170/274 ⑥
mph/kmh ❷ gear
SENNA
HILL 180/290 ⑥
45/72
SCHUMACHER
PROST
STEWART 130/209 ①
ASCARI 70/113 ③

RACE CLASSIFICATION

Pos	Driver	Nat	Car	Laps	Time
1	Michael Schumacher	D	Ferrari F2001-Ferrari V10	58	1h38m26.533s
2	David Coulthard	GB	McLaren MP4-16-Mercedes V10	58	+1.718s
3	Rubens Barrichello	BR	Ferrari F2001-Ferrari V10	58	+33.491s
4	Nick Heidfeld	D	Sauber C20-Petronas V10	58	+1m11.479s
5	Heinz-Harald Frentzen	D	Jordan EJ11-Honda V10	58	+1m12.807s
6	Kimi Raikkonen	FIN	Sauber C20-Petronas V10	58	+1m24.143s
7	Olivier Panis	F	BAR 003-Honda V10	58	+1m27.050s
8	Luciano Burti	BR	Jaguar R2-Ford Cosworth V10		+1 lap
9	Jos Verstappen	NL	Arrows A22-Asiatech V10		+1 lap
10	Jean Alesi	F	Prost AP04-Acer V10		+1 lap
11	Eddie Irvine	GB	Jaguar R2-Ford Cosworth V10		+1 lap
12	Fernando Alonso	E	Minardi PS01-European V10		+2 laps
13	Giancarlo Fisichella	I	Benetton B201-Renault V10		+3 laps
14	Jenson Button	GB	Benetton B201-Renault V10		+6 laps

Retirements	Nat	Car	Laps	Reason
Juan Pablo Montoya	CO	Williams FW23-BMW V10	40	engine
Jarno Trulli	I	Jordan EJ11-Honda V10	38	engine misfire
Mika Hakkinen	FIN	McLaren MP4-16-Mercedes V10	25	front susp. / accident
Ralf Schumacher	D	Williams FW23-BMW V10	4	accident
Jacques Villeneuve	CDN	BAR 003-Honda V10	4	accident
Tarso Marques	BR	Minardi PS01-European V10	3	battery
Enrique Bernoldi	BR	Arrows A22-Asiatech V10	2	accident
Gaston Mazzacane	RA	Prost AP04-Acer V10	0	brake pedal

Olivier Panis finished fourth but was relegated for overtaking under yellow flags

FASTEST LAP M Schumacher 1m28.214s lap 34 (134.474mph / 216.415kmh)

DRIVERS' CHAMPIONSHIP

1	Michael Schumacher	10
2	David Coulthard	6
3	Rubens Barrichello	4
4	Nick Heidfeld	3
5	Heinz-Harald Frentzen	2
6	Kimi Raikkonen	1

CONSTRUCTORS' CHAMPIONSHIP

1	Ferrari	14
2	McLaren-Mercedes	6
3	Sauber-Petronas	4
4	Jordan-Honda	2

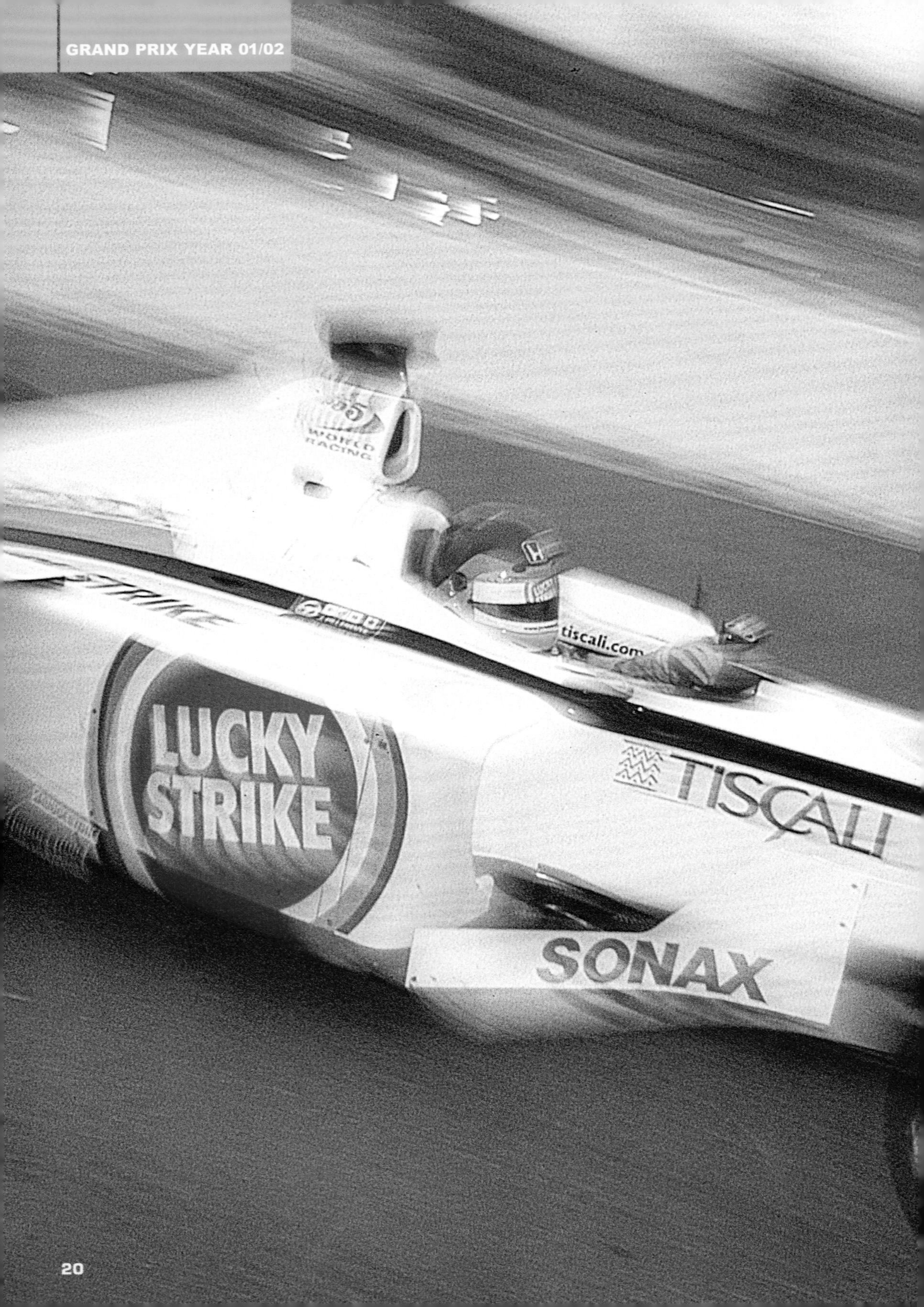
LUCKY STRIKE
TISCALI
SONAX
tiscali.com

DON'T LOOK BACK IN ANGER

LUCKY STRIKE B.A.R HONDA MIGHT NOT HAVE ACHIEVED ITS TARGETS IN 2001, BUT AMBITION REMAINS INTACT. A TOUGH CAMPAIGN HAS MADE THE TEAM'S BOSS EVEN MORE DETERMINED TO SUCCEED, IF THAT WERE POSSIBLE

SINCE THE TEAM'S CONCEPTION IN 1998, BRITISH American Racing has set its standards high. Very high. Last year, major upgrades to their prestigious Technical Centre in Brackley, Northamptonshire brought them on a˙ level with the likes of Ferrari, McLaren and Williams. The new multi-million dollar wind tunnel, and similar commitments in research and development laid a strong foundation for the 2001 season. A new engine deal secured works Honda power, linked to the strengths of the 1997 world champion, Jacques Villeneuve. Winners both, with a total commitment to success.

The 350-strong B.A.R staff is now both highly respected and motivated. Their race budget from the generous British American Tobacco sponsorship ensures them a seat at Formula One's top table. So with all the elements seemingly in place, what are we to make of a season with such mixed fortunes?

Following an indifferent start to the team's GP career, Lucky Strike B.A.R Honda got their collective heads down in 2000 to produce some excellent results and fully justify their place in the GP paddock. The portents were good. The team was buoyant.

On the back of that second term's success, Lucky Strike B.A.R Honda billed year three – or 2001 – as the "quality evolution". What transpired was a year of digging deep; re-engineering both its product and its goals. The BAR 003, as the 2001 chassis was known, lacked the development required to compete at the highest echelon of the sport and, in a sport that is played out so close to the margins, such small differences proved to be key. No single aspect of the BAR 003 was actually "off the mark", but the sum of its parts just wasn't enough to mount a serious challenge to the likes of Ferrari, McLaren and Williams as had been hoped.

Lucky Strike B.A.R Honda is packed with perfectionists – and bad losers. They take their lead from managing director and team principal, Craig Pollock. Only wins and podiums were ever going to be good enough this year. But no matter how quickly Lucky Strike B.A.R Honda set its personal fast-track, that sort of target is a big ask for any infant team. Perhaps then, expectations were running just too high?

"Yes – but this only became clear towards mid-season," says Pollock. "We agreed objectives based upon the results of last season but we believe that every team should start the season with lofty ambitions. We certainly underestimated how much other teams were going to develop; particularly how much the older and more experienced teams would raise their game in 2001. The introduction of manufacturers and the injection of huge funding have made a big difference to the sport. All the more reason to fight and continue to develop. It gives me no satisfaction in saying this, but it became apparent that by Silverstone we were midfield runners with a slightly stronger showing in the races. Yes, it is only year three and yes, we were reliable but we came to win.

So why didn't they? Well, Lucky Strike B.A.R Honda sent out the right messages at the start of the year by strengthening the team with some high-calibre additions. On the driver front, Olivier Panis breezed into Brackley as an experienced replacement for Ricardo Zonta. The 1996 Monaco GP winner brought much needed on-track knowledge to both race and test teams and as Pollock openly declared he would do, put pressure on Villeneuve for much of the season. But JV reacted well to the Frenchman's arrival. The duo formed an excellent relationship throughout the year, despite Panis being JV's most competitive team-mate since Damon Hill in 1996.

The test driver line-up was expanded too. Stalwarts Darren Manning and Patrick Lemarié were retained and two very hot newcomers – Takuma Sato and Anthony Davidson – assisted them. For good measure the Lucky Strike B.A.R Honda young guns also teamed up in the prestigious British Formula Three Championship, which they completely dominated. And although it was Sato who took the title, time might show that the maturity of 22-year-old Davidson, who was in his first year in F3, will pay off in F1.

Meanwhile, inside the garage, the highly respected James Robinson joined the team as chief race engineer from Williams.

So with two GP winners in the cockpit and many seasoned campaigners within the team, the crux of the problem for Lucky Strike B.A.R Honda in 2001 was clearly the performance of the car. The BAR 003 combined two years of development by the team and Honda's considerable F1 nous. Allied to a far greater emphasis on detail, the quality of finish and a new Lucky Strike livery, the BAR 003 certainly looked the part and should have been very good. But like a lot of marriages, it needed time to mature – something the team had to learn the hard way in 2001.

The year started with testing in Barcelona. Even then Villeneuve had suspicions that things were not at the required level.

Performance was lacking and he took no pleasure in letting the team know. By the time the team reached Australia for the first race, many revisions had been made.

Come the opening race, the laconic, likeable Olivier Panis, who had settled easily in the team, almost grabbed a podium visit first time out. He was eventually edged into fourth by Rubens Barrichello, then knocked further back by the FIA after the race. They ruled he'd overtaken Nick Heidfeld's Sauber under yellow flags. A 25-second penalty meant his well-earned fourth became a hard-to-swallow seventh and no points.

Olivier just shrugged his shoulders at the disappointment and went on to grab the team's first points of the year two races later in Brazil, despite a problematic pit stop. This time the result stood and gave the Frenchman his first points since the 1999 German GP.

The first major overhaul to the BAR 003 came in time for the return to Europe. In the San Marino and Spanish GPs the team used a completely new aerodynamic package and a revised exhaust system. This improved the power delivery while reducing the operating temperatures of the rear suspension and lower rear wing. The results were good.

Jacques hadn't fared quite as well as his team-mate from the kick-off. He suffered six DNFs all season, but half of them came in his first four races. With all the style and gusto we have come to expect from the Canadian, he bounced back to take his first points of the season with a podium in Barcelona. Okay, it was a lucky strike – Mika Hakkinen's McLaren packing up on the final lap allowed JV through to gatecrash the rostrum – but it was reward at last for Villeneuve's perseverance and the hard-working Lucky Strike B.A.R Honda team. After all the cynicism and criticism that had gone before, no one could deny the B.A.R boys and girls their moment. Celebrations were well deserved and lasted long into the morning.

ON A TRACK THAT HAD PLAGUED VILLENEUVE IN 2000, HE LOOKED VERY GOOD ALL AFTERNOON AND CAME HOME FOURTH

ACTION MEN, clockwise from left: team boss Craig Pollock; Villeneuve leads Alesi's Jordan – the battle between the two Honda teams was settled on an FIA technicality; overhead view of this year's model; Villeneuve on the podium in Spain; pit brief for JV

Visibly lifted by his return to eminence, JV followed up an overly determined effort for no points in Austria with probably the best Lucky Strike B.A.R Honda performance of the season. The team, looking to capitalise on this upturn in fortunes and to meet the unique challenge of Monte Carlo's streets, took a new front wing and diffuser to Monaco. Again it worked well. Villeneuve was able to throw the car around the tight street circuit with great aplomb. On a track that had plagued Villeneuve in 2000, he looked very good all afternoon and came home fourth, stuck to the tail of Irvine's Jaguar. It was a masterly display of driving around the toughest GP circuit of them all and a reminder, if any was needed, of why he became world champion in the first place. Class is permanent.

But while this patch of the season was tinted purple, it didn't last. The races from Canada through to Britain all proved problematic and, despite the best efforts of Lucky Strike B.A.R Honda's overworked team, the car wouldn't play ball. Plus, the competition was hotting up. The car was proving less competitive and the drivers felt the pressure. Villeneuve's first-corner lunge that dismissed his team-mate at the British GP summed up the

23

mid-season malaise perfectly.

Understandably, the team arrived for the German GP on a real downer. But although there were only a few technical tinkerings made to the car, they found a superb race set-up. Lucky Strike B.A.R Honda went on to secure its second podium of the year, thanks to another vintage Villeneuve performance. Tenacious, quick and off the cuff, he came home in third to defy the formbook. Spare a thought too for the charging Panis, who on a two-stop strategy, was desperately unlucky to finish a place outside the points after a similarly sublime drive.

Unfortunately, that success proved to be only a temporary respite and the following races proved to be character-building. No matter what the team introduced throughout the remainder of the season and no matter how many hours they put in behind the scenes, Villeneuve and Panis were unable to scale such heights again. The team responded for the Hungarian and Belgian Grands Prix with a constant, round-the-clock effort to upgrade the car, but further success was not to be.

JUDGING FROM THE RHETORIC, POLLOCK WILL BE ADOPTING A MORE HANDS-ON ROLE TO INSPIRE HIS STAFF TO GREATER THINGS

The Italian Grand Prix at Monza went ahead despite the terrorist attacks on America only a few days before. Minds were understandably elsewhere, but JV retained his focus to grab what proved to be the team's last point of the season. He also stole the headlines for defying Michael Schumacher and his attempted driver's coup that sought to ban overtaking through the notorious Prima Variante chicane on lap one. "I'm a racing driver and I'm going to race." said Villeneuve. "It was a question of principles I've had since I was a boy dreaming of being a racing driver. I believe you have to go flat out from the start and give 100 per cent to the chequered flag." Enough said.

The penultimate race of the year at an obviously sombre Indianapolis proved to be the season's nadir for Lucky Strike B.A.R Honda. The team tried out new rear wing formations, but was already looking ahead and developing next year's car. Villeneuve looked like he would rather be somewhere else; he qualified in a career-low 18th place and finished his race in the pits after a coming together with Pedro de la Rosa. Not even the consistent Panis managed to find a scrap in the dog's dinner that day.

"The US Grand Prix was our worst racing performance of the last three seasons and I was embarrassed," admitted team boss Pollock afterwards. Villeneuve took most of the criticism on the chin and acknowledged a lot of it was justified.

Such frankness and honesty are rare commodities in today's F1 paddock and there is no doubt that this rallying cry stirred his troops into action for the seasonal finale at Suzuka. Despite a customarily difficult qualifying session Villeneuve, in particular, drove like a man possessed. In the end his efforts couldn't secure valuable championship points, but for Pollock, it was exactly the reaction he was looking for. There is no doubt that in the overall scheme of things, this was much more important to him than beating Jordan for the Honda laurels – a battle that would eventually be lost not on the race track, but in an FIA courtroom two weeks

STRIKE FORCE: awaiting the start in America (left); Panis (centre left) made a strong return after a year's F1 sabbatical; JV faces the media scrum (centre right); Villeneuve leads Panis in Hungary (bottom)

after the end of the season. Craig Pollock had cracked the whip and got an immediate response. Now he has something to work with over the winter.

So the end-of-year report for Lucky Strike B.A.R Honda reflects a team that soldiered diligently all season to make the most of a car that was not as developed as it needed to be. In mitigation, the car was always very reliable in race trim. But it badly needed a boost in qualifying guise, because the best Villeneuve or Panis could extract from it all year was sixth on the grid. Moreover, the two Lucky Strike B.A.R Honda drivers' average qualifying spot slipped into double figures as the year unfolded and that is a considerable handicap to carry into any race.

However, the lowest point of this – or any other – year came in Australia, when Jacques Villeneuve collided with Ralf Schumacher's Williams at 185mph. Villeneuve's car was sent skywards, then cartwheeled into before coming to a halt. Incredibly he was uninjured. Track marshal Graham Beveridge was less fortunate. The 51-year-old Queenslander was tragically killed by flying debris.

The terrible accident was the worst possible beginning to the year for all in F1. Make no mistake; Beveridge's death affected Jacques and the Lucky Strike B.A.R Honda team very badly indeed.

But after all the problems of 2001, what is needed to really turn things around? What can Craig Pollock do to boost the Lucky Strike B.A.R Honda effort?

Judging from the rhetoric emerging from Brackley at the end of the year, Pollock will be adopting a more hands-on role to inspire his staff to greater things. He will make whatever changes are necessary to succeed and insist on greater efforts from his drivers, staff, technical partners and suppliers.

As a team, British American Racing knows it must deliver in 2002. In a year when Honda looks likely to choose bed partners for the foreseeable future, and co-owner and title sponsor British American Tobacco will want to quantify its huge three-year investment, significant progress is a must. But with the promised technical support and earlier development of the new car, it is a challenge Lucky Strike B.A.R Honda is up for and seems capable of making.

Pollock acknowledges that the team's credibility might have slipped towards the end of 2001, but whatever the outside perspective of Lucky Strike B.A.R Honda, Pollock's own determination remains undiluted. "No one person can turn things around," he says, "it is a team effort. I intend to ensure that we have a strengthened package in place well in advance of the start of the next season. I will not accept anything less than a race-winning package. I expect to get the best from the team and the drivers at each and every race. We are a team full of youthful energy and expertise with a huge passion for what we do. Lucky Strike B.A.R Honda wants to be successful – the team wants to win. The buck stops with every single individual. We are all accountable – especially me – and no stone will be left unturned to make sure we act like a team with championship ambitions."

No more Mr Nice Guy, then. This is a man on a mission, king of a team still hurting for success. ■

PETRONAS MALAYSIAN GRAND PRIX

THE BAD NEWS? SCHUEY WENT FLYING ACROSS THE GRASS DURING A VIOLENT DOWNPOUR AND SPENT MORE THAN A MINUTE CHANGING TYRES AFTER FERRARI GOT IN A SPLENDID MUDDLE. THE GOOD NEWS? IT DIDN'T MATTER, BECAUSE HE WAS THAT MUCH FASTER THAN THE REST. THAT'LL BE SIX OUT OF SIX, THEN

FIST AMONG EQUALS: Schuey in triumphal mood (right) after an easy day at the office. If the photographer had hung around for another 20 seconds or so, he might have caught Barrichello on film, too. Above, Coulthard (right) gets close to the Ferrari drivers — the only time during the afternoon that he managed to do so

A FAINT VOICE COULD JUST BE HEARD OVER THE
Benetton team's intercom: "Ooops. Sorry."

It came from Giancarlo Fisichella – who was almost as lost on the grid as his team had become trying to sort out the recalcitrant B201. Bizarrely, the Italian completely forgot where he was supposed to line up and, having tried in vain to rectify the mess, he ended up straddling the circuit.

Abort start, player one. Fisichella, go to the back of the grid.

Take two. . . and this time Juan Pablo Montoya was the one left feeling stranded as his engine died. While the rest of the field trailed around behind pole-winner Michael Schumacher's Ferrari on the formation lap, Montoya hopped over the pit wall and jumped in the spare Williams, which was ready in time for him to start from the end of the pit lane.

It might have been an all-Ferrari front row, but it was a one-Prancing Horse race to the first corner. As Schuey – who made a late switch to the team spare when his own chassis developed an oil leak – set about stamping his authority on the afternoon, his younger brother's Williams outgunned Rubens Barrichello and slipped around the outside as they peeled into the first turn. Just as Rubens had done unto Heinz-Harald Frentzen in Australia, however, he did unto Schuey Jnr this time. A tap on the rear corner sent the Williams spinning round and Ralf rejoined at the back. Rubens? He carried on in second, ahead of Jarno Trulli and David Coulthard. Robust as well as rapid, those Ferraris.

COME ON YOU REDS: the Ferraris prepare to swamp Trulli (right). This was also the moment when Barrichello came over all mard because Schuey passed him, too. Face facts, Rubens, it was always going to happen. Inset, Jos the Boss – funny description of someone who finished seventh

WATER BORED: the Jordan pit crew in action (below) on the Kuala Lumpur Ship Canal

SILVER BARROWS: the McLarens were approximately nowhere, although Coulthard (below right) salvaged third

WHEN THEY EMERGED, BEHIND THE SAFETY CAR, COULTHARD LED FROM FRENTZEN AND JOS VERSTAPPEN (LOOKS LIKE IT OUGHT TO BE A MISPRINT, BUT ISN'T)

The race might have started in dry weather, but earlier in the day there had been a seasonal monsoon – and another was about to strike.

On lap two Olivier Panis spun his BAR – not because of rain, but because his Honda had gone bang and spewed oil all over the rear tyres. . . and the track. It was moments later that the day's second deluge began in earnest, leastways on part of the track.

When the two Ferraris arrived at Turn Six (evocative name, guys) on lap four, they were aware of the rain, less so of Panis's Honda lubricant. Both went skittering across the grass. Farther back, Trulli and Coulthard spotted the Ferrari pantomime and had time to brake sufficiently early to make it round the corner unimpeded. Before the lap was out, however, the rain would intensify and they, too, skated off before rejoining.

Running at the back of the field, Montoya was first to radio in and ask for wet tyres to be made ready. Williams was geared up to welcome Schuey Jnr, however, and told Juan Pablo to stay out. He did – and became beached in the gravel before he made it back. The downpour also brought about the permanent downfall of Jacques Villeneuve, Enrique Bernoldi and Nick Heidfeld, while all survivors paddled around as best they could before pitting to change tyres. When they emerged, behind the Safety Car, Coulthard led from Frentzen, Jos Verstappen's Arrows (looks like

TRACTION MAN

It was oppressive in Malaysia – more than 90 degrees even mid-rainstorm – but during the build-up to the race no one was feeling the heat quite as much as Heinz-Harald Frentzen.

The information superhighway can be a wonderful thing, but he was beginning to wish the media hadn't logged on to www.frentzen.de, his personal website, to read what he had said in the wake of the Australian GP.

Having duelled with the Saubers in Melbourne, Frentzen wrote: "I don't know if traction control comes as a factory option with Ferrari engines, but every time I got close in a slower corner he (Nick Heidfeld) would pull away under acceleration, which was strange as I could hear the engine misfiring!"

An audible misfire, of course, was a characteristic of old-fashioned traction control systems before they were banned at the end of 1993. Under hostile questioning, Frentzen remained calm. "The problem," he said, "is that my remarks were taken out of context. I never said anyone was cheating, but there is a way for teams to control traction within the regulations. If anyone bothered reading all the articles on my site they would know this."

While it was illegal to have a device that reacted to wheelspin, it was feasible to run a system that predicted when it might occur and thus throttled back in anticipation. A subtle difference, but a difference all the same. And legal.

Frentzen took time to explain all this – and did so eloquently. As he finished, a journalist rose (from his slumbers, apparently) to ask: "So why did you say Ferrari–engined cars were cheating?"

Frentzen just shook his head in quiet, understandable disbelief.

CHARGE OF THE LATE BRIGADE: Hakkinen monsters Schuey Jnr after waking up

HAKKINEN'S SPURT NETTED FASTEST LAP – BUT BY THEN IT WAS TOO LITTLE, TOO LATE

it ought to be a misprint, but isn't), Mika Hakkinen, Trulli, Jean Alesi, Giancarlo Fisichella, Schuey Jnr (mildly reprieved after gaining ground during the stops), Gaston Mazzacane and the Ferraris of Barrichello and Schuey Snr.

Everyone opted for wet tyres. . . apart from the two men driving red cars, who were 10th and 11th after stops that took longer then scheduled because Barrichello pitted first, after overtaking his team-mate while both were on the grass. The team had been expecting Schuey and thus had Michael's tyres sitting on the pit apron. They might have got their sets muddled up, but at least they had the compound right. The Ferrari duo had tried intermediate tyres during the warm-up and felt them to be ultra-effective even in the wet. Nobody had predicted, however, that they might be about four seconds per lap more effective.

The pair of them screamed through the field at an extraordinary rate. Schuey paused briefly behind Barrichello before squeezing by with an opportunist move that infuriated the Brazilian, who thought it a touch over-aggressive in the conditions. Only Verstappen, doing an admirable job in the nimble Arrows, held the German up for more than a couple of nanoseconds.

There was inevitably talk that traction control was on view a touch before its scheduled reintroduction in Barcelona, but rivals appeared unconcerned. Patrick Head, technical director of Williams, said: "They were on different tyres – and I expect that would explain the gulf in performance."

At the start of lap 16 Schuey swept past Coulthard to take the lead and Barrichello followed through soon afterwards. Job done. "I think you are seeing a very good Ferrari against a not-quite-sorted McLaren," Coulthard said after trailing home almost half a minute behind Schuey, for whom this was a sixth straight win. The last time anybody put together a run like that was in 1952/53, when Alberto Ascari bagged nine on the trot for Ferrari.

Frentzen, Schuey Jnr and Hakkinen scored the remaining points, although Hakkinen scarcely deserved one. He spent much of the race bottled up behind Verstappen's Arrows but only once tried to pass it. When the Finn finally got ahead, courtesy of a pit stop reshuffle, he remembered what he is paid to do and set after Schuey Jnr with a vengeance. His spurt netted fastest lap, but by then it was too little, too late. ∎

OUT OF THE FRYING SEPANG

You could barely move for promotional hoardings in and around the Sepang circuit – but for most of the weekend there was plenty of space on the spectator banks.

Opened in 1999, close to Kuala Lumpur international airport (about one hour by road from KL, although the city is expanding at such a rate that it should reach the airport within a couple of years), the track puts many European venues to shame. Teams have a selection of powerfully air-conditioned units in which to take refuge and most grandstands offer a terrific view.

But with the Malaysian GP moving to the beginning of the season, rather than its former slot at the end, this was the country's second F1 race in the space of five months. And herein lay the problem.

Many Malaysians earn less in a month than Michael Schumacher makes in one lap, hence the initial paucity of ticket sales. Things picked up a little on raceday, but you didn't exactly have to queue to get in.

One local fan admitted that he had planned to climb over the fence to watch the race – except that he couldn't do that because he would have been charged the local equivalent of about £1.80 to park his bicycle at the spot where he planned to carry out his felony. And he couldn't afford that, either.

ACCESS RATING FOR BRITS ★★
Sure, it's a lot nearer than Melbourne – but we're still talking 13 hours of having to put up with airline staff giving you false smiles. And staying in Kuala Lumpur might be desirable, but it's not terribly practical.

STARTING GRID

1 M Schumacher
1m35.220s

2 Barrichello
1m35.319s

5 R Schumacher
1m35.511s

3 Hakkinen
1m36.040s

12 Trulli
1m36.180s

6 Montoya
1m36.218s

10 Villeneuve
1m 36.397s

4 Coulthard
1m36.417s

11 Frentzen
1m36.578s

9 Panis
1m36.681s

16 Heidfeld
1m36.913s

18 Irvine
1m37.140s

22 Alesi
1m37.406s

17 Raikkonen
1m37.728s

19 Burti
1m38.035s

7 Fisichella
1m38.086s

8 Button
1m38.258s

14 Verstappen
1m38.509s

23 Mazzacane
1m39.006s

20 Marques
1m39.714s

21 Alonso
1m40.249s

15 Bernoldi
0m0.000s

Bernoldi qualified 19th but his time was disallowed due to a rear wing infringement

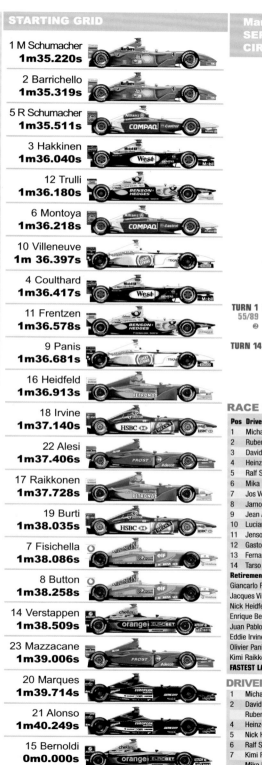

March 18 2001
SEPANG CIRCUIT, KUALA LUMPUR
CIRCUIT LENGTH: 3.444miles / 5.543km

mph/kmh
❷ gear

TURN 4
65/105
❷

TURN 6
130/209
❹

TURN 7
100/161
❹

TURN 15
50/81
❷

TURN 5
130/209❹

TURN 3
140/225
❹

TURN 8
100/161
❹

180/290
❹

TURN 2

TURN 9
40/64
❶

TURN 10

TURN 1
55/89
❷

TURN 12

130/209❹

TURN 14

TURN 11
80/129
❸

TURN 13
65/105❷

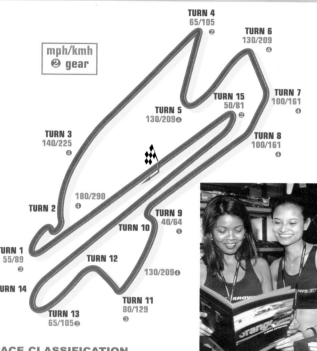

RACE CLASSIFICATION

Pos	Driver	Nat	Car	Laps	Time
1	Michael Schumacher	D	Ferrari F2001–Ferrari V10	55	1h47m34.801s
2	Rubens Barrichello	BR	Ferrari F2001–Ferrari V10	55	+23.660s
3	David Coulthard	GB	McLaren MP4–16–Mercedes V10	55	+28.555s
4	Heinz–Harald Frentzen	D	Jordan EJ11–Honda V10	55	+46.543s
5	Ralf Schumacher	D	Williams FW23–BMW V10	55	+48.233s
6	Mika Hakkinen	FIN	McLaren MP4–16–Mercedes V10	55	+48.606s
7	Jos Verstappen	NL	Arrows A22–Asiatech V10	55	+1m21.560s
8	Jarno Trulli	I	Jordan EJ11–Honda V10		+1 lap
9	Jean Alesi	F	Prost AP04–Acer V10		+1 lap
10	Luciano Burti	BR	Jaguar R2–Ford Cosworth V10		+1 lap
11	Jenson Button	GB	Benetton B201–Renault V10		+2 laps
12	Gaston Mazzacane	RA	Prost AP04–Acer V10		+2 laps
13	Fernando Alonso	E	Minardi PS01–European V10		+3 laps
14	Tarso Marques	BR	Minardi PS01–European V10		+4 laps
Retirements		**Nat**	**Car**	**Laps**	**Reason**
	Giancarlo Fisichella	I	Benetton B201–Renault V10	31	fuel pump
	Jacques Villeneuve	CDN	BAR 003–Honda V10	3	spin
	Nick Heidfeld	D	Sauber C20–Petronas V10	3	spin
	Enrique Bernoldi	BR	Arrows A22–Asiatech V10	3	spin
	Juan Pablo Montoya	CO	Williams FW23–BMW V10	3	spin
	Eddie Irvine	GB	Jaguar R2–Ford Cosworth V10	3	accident / radiator
	Olivier Panis	F	BAR 003–Honda V10	1	oil system / engine fire
	Kimi Raikkonen	FIN	Sauber C20–Petronas V10	0	transmission
FASTEST LAP			**M Hakkinen 1m40.962s lap 48 (122.812mph / 197.647kmh)**		

DRIVERS' CHAMPIONSHIP

1	Michael Schumacher	20
2	David Coulthard	10
	Rubens Barrichello	10
4	Heinz–Harald Frentzen	5
5	Nick Heidfeld	3
6	Ralf Schumacher	2
7	Kimi Raikkonen	1
	Mika Hakkinen	1

CONSTRUCTORS' CHAMPIONSHIP

1	Ferrari	30
2	McLaren–Mercedes	11
3	Jordan–Honda	5
4	Sauber–Petronas	4
5	Williams–BMW	2

THIS YEAR'S MODELS

FORMULA ONE IS AT THE CUTTING EDGE OF ALMOST EVERYTHING . . . APART, PERHAPS, FROM POLITICAL CORRECTNESS. COME RAIN, SHINE OR AUSTRIAN SLIME, SOME POOR SAPS HAVE TO TURN OUT WEARING THINGS THAT CONTAIN JUST ABOUT ENOUGH MATERIAL TO MAKE HALF A BIKINI. HERE IS SOME OF THE EVIDENCE FOR THE PROSECUTION

1

PEACH MELBOURNE: Sacrilege (1) – the only things that should be allowed to wear blue and orange in a motor racing paddock are the Ford GT40 and Porsche 917. This lot were in Australia to promote the supporting V8 touring car race. Red wigs – not funny in 2000, still not funny in 2001 (2). Stop it, all of you. Jordan didn't have much to smile about last season, but there were exceptions (3). Malaysian national costume (4) really ought to include an umbrella. All over BAR the pouting (5). Grid girl laughs at Eddie Irvine's suggestion that he's second best in the world (6). The latest F1 tyres generate enough heat to make a half-decent sunbed (7). Psychology A-level, question one: "You are paid a fortune to focus on driving a grand prix car at your full potential. How are you supposed to concentrate when someone sticks an arse in tight red leather trousers (8) right in front of your car on the grid?"

8

GRANDE PREMIO MARLBORO DO BRASI

ALBERTO ASCARI'S LONG-STANDING RECORD OF NINE STRAIGHT F1 WINS IS NO LONGER UNDER THREAT AS SCHUMACHER IS OUT-SCHUMACHERED TWICE IN THE SPACE OF 40-ODD LAPS. MONTOYA STARS – BUT COULTHARD WINS

WEST HAMMER: it looks a bit like the cover of a prog rock album, circa 1972, but it is in fact Coulthard splashing to victory (main shot). Above, Montoya was unofficial winner of the race's dry bit.

IN YEARS TO COME WE WILL PROBABLY LOOK back on this as one of Formula One's defining moments.

The first corner. Brazil 2001. Lap three. On the right there was Michael Schumacher – professionally uncompromising, known to be hard and fast in equal measure. On the left? Juan Pablo Montoya – making only his third grand prix start, utterly fearless and potentially faster than lightning.

The world was looking forward to seeing the two of them compete on equal terms – and the moment didn't take too long coming.

The build-up was as follows. Schumacher started smartly from pole, but his younger brother, alongside, was not so alert. Mika Hakkinen, third on the grid, went absolutely nowhere and Montoya sprinted into second place.

Hakkinen was sufficiently steamed up about stalling that he flounced away from his car and forgot to reattach the steering wheel (which has to be unclipped to let drivers get in and out). This made it somewhat tricky for marshals to shift the stricken McLaren, so the Safety Car consequently emerged for two laps and Hakkinen was fined $5,000 (aka about as much as he earns in a couple of hours).

At the restart, Montoya drafted up behind Schuey on the run to the first corner and Michael moved left to close the door. The Colombian saw it closing but kept coming until finally Schumacher recognised a kindred spirit looming and jinked right. The two cars all but kissed wheels and Schuey wobbled over the kerbs as Montoya sped through and away. One-nil Colombia.

Thereafter Michael stayed with the leader for a bit, but Montoya drove faultlessly and kept him at bay – even though he was driving a heavier car, with a one-stop fuel load to the Ferrari's two. Once Schuey had pitted for the first time, Montoya was a distant blip on the radar, about half a minute up the road.

The German couldn't see the leader – but neither, apparently, could Jos Verstappen. He might have driven magnificently in Malaysia, but here the Dutchman was

TOUCHING A ROAR NERVE: Jaguar's back-to-basics approach was supposed to favour durability over speed – but in Brazil neither quality was evident. Irvine (below) spun off in the deluge. Right (from the left, if that makes sense): Schuey and DC wonder how Nick Heidfeld can reach the pedals; Montoya shows the world champ how it should be done; and Alesi plays TCR jammer car

half-asleep. No, make that totally asleep. Montoya was on his 39th circuit, and contemplating a fuel stop, when he lapped Verstappen. Jos moved over obligingly, then pulled back across the road and simply plunged into the back of the leader as they reached Turn Four. Both were out on the spot.

Montoya grinned through the pain, however. He knew he'd made his point. "I don't know what Verstappen was playing at," he said. "It should have been one of the best days of my life, and then bang. It wasn't to be." The FIA was smiling, too, because its coffers swelled by another $10,000 courtesy of a fine slapped on Verstappen.

This was very much a race of two halves. The first belonged to Montoya, the second to David Coulthard. The Scot vaulted into third at the start – and had a couple of potential predators removed when Rubens

THE TWO CARS ALL BUT KISSED WHEELS AND SCHUEY WOBBLED OVER THE KERBS AS MONTOYA SPED THROUGH AND AWAY

HOME BLEAK HOME

Brazil expects – and has been doing so for quite some time.

Spoiled by the successes of Emerson Fittipaldi, Nelson Piquet and Ayrton Senna through the Seventies, Eighties and early Nineties, the nation has come to believe that motor racing glory is its by right. Since Senna's death at Imola in 1994, however, the Brazilian national anthem has been played only once at the end of a grand prix, when Rubens Barrichello won at Hockenheim in 2000.

As always there was a sea of red T-shirts and Ferrari flags in the crowd, but the commentator's persistently wild efforts to cajole the crowd into chanting Barrichello's name brought a slightly muted response, almost as if the fans expected their man to be given a good duffing by his team-mate.

"Rubinho" duly qualified sixth, five places behind Schumacher M, but he thought his luck might have changed when his designated race car packed up on the formation lap because of failing oil pressure. Better for it to happen then, he reasoned, than lap one of the race.

Rubens jogged along close to the side of the track for a while, then cadged a lift in a clapped-out van before making it back to the pits in time to take the spare chassis. Barely had the race begun in anger, however, than he had clumsily ploughed into Ralf Schumacher's Williams.

Of the four Brazilians in the field, only Tarso Marques finished – and he was ninth, three laps down (rather less electrifying than the storm that followed the race).

Before the F1 circus moved into town, police had taken time clearing stray dogs away from the Interlagos track. "The first one they picked up was nicknamed Rubinho," one local said, "because he was slow and easy to catch."

NO DROUGHT ABOUT IT: Heidfeld's podium finish was Sauber's first since Hungary '97

RUBBER AND BULLETS

NICK HEIDFELD ENDORSED HIS GROWING REPUTATION BY PICKING HIS WAY THROUGH THE RACE OF A THOUSAND SPINS TO COLLECT A MAGNIFICENT THIRD

Barrichello torpedoed into Schuey Jnr within moments of the Safety Car peeling in. He retired, while the German had to pit for a new rear wing and would later spin off.

With Schuey Snr having refuelled, Verstappen's gauche manoeuvre handed Coulthard the lead – and he kept it, just, after making his only scheduled stop on lap 40.

And then it rained. It was light at first, but a full-on tropical downpour commenced on lap 46. Schuey dived straight in for a set of the Bridgestone intermediates that had allowed him to marmalise the opposition in Sepang, but before opting for the same Coulthard stayed out for an extra, ultra-slippery lap.

This looked like a very poor decision, but he was still within striking distance of Schuey when he rejoined – and then Michael unexpectedly performed a half-spin. The Scot was right on his tail at the end of lap 49 when they entered the main straight, where up ahead Tarso Marques's Minardi was plodding along, several millennia off the pace. The leaders passed either side, Schuey to Marques's right and Coulthard to the left. As they swept into the first turn Coulthard emerged ahead and proceeded to drive away from Michael as though he, too, were in a Minardi.

Schumacher's winning run was over. And Coulthard justly rated this as one of his finest performances (as you would if you'd just outperformed Schuey in the wet). "We compromised the set-up a little to account for the rain we were expecting," he said. "It didn't cause many problems at the start of the race and in the damp the car worked really well. This is the best feeling I've ever had from a grand prix victory."

Schuey came home a grumpy second and Nick Heidfeld endorsed his growing reputation by picking his way through the race of a thousand spins to collect a magnificent third for Sauber, albeit one lap down. He was helped by a cornucopia of problems that afflicted the Jordans, Jaguars and BARs, but it was a fine drive nonetheless. Olivier Panis and Jarno Trulli were next across the line, while others' woes allowed Giancarlo Fisichella to pick up an improbable point for Benetton. ∎

Interlagos. Fleapit or international sporting arena? Discuss.

The Brazilian GP's host track leaves few people indifferent. The majority appear to hate it. Some F1 folk even decline to go.

Last year advertising hoardings had an unfortunate tendency to fall over and land on the track; this time a remote pit lane camera toppled from its mountings and crashed down in the Jaguar pit. That no one was hurt was a product of pure luck (it took four men to lift it away afterwards).

And things are even worse outside the circuit's perimeter walls. Plant something as conspicuously cash-rich as F1 in the middle of a Sao Paulo suburb where poverty and crime are rife, and the atmosphere is inevitably edgy. A Minardi employee was set upon and robbed after making a cash withdrawal from a bank; an armed gunman approached a Williams minibus on its way to the track one morning; laptop computers were stolen from the Jaguar pit; Minardi had a pile of wheels nicked.

In its defence, Interlagos has a tumbledown charm. That's not much of a defence, true, but some circuits are more about presentation that product – beautifully laid out and with all the facilities you could need, but frankly crap when it comes to promoting good racing. Interlagos is the other way around – a great track layout, but about as state-of-the-art as a council skip.

ACCESS RATING FOR BRITS *
Takes bloody ages to fly there, the circuit won't be finished when you arrive, the traffic is three times as bad as London's and you need to be exceedingly prudent at all times.

STARTING GRID

1 M Schumacher
1m13.780s

5 R Schumacher
1m14.090s

3 Hakkinen
1m14.122s

6 Montoya
1m14.165s

4 Coulthard
1m14.178s

2 Barrichello
1m14.191s

12 Trulli
1m14.630s

11 Frentzen
1m14.633s

16 Heidfeld
1m14.810s

17 Raikkonen
1m14.924s

9 Panis
1m15.046s

10 Villeneuve
1m15.182s

18 Irvine
1m15.192s

19 Burti
1m15.371s

22 Alesi
1m15.437s

15 Bernoldi
1m15.657s

14 Verstappen
1m15.704s

7 Fisichella
1m16.175s

21 Alonso
1m16.184s

8 Button
1m16.229s

23 Mazzacane
1m16.520s

20 Marques
1m16.784s

April 1 2001
AUTODROMO JOSÉ CARLOS PACE, INTERLAGOS, SAO PAULO. CIRCUIT LENGTH: 2.677miles / 4.309km

mph/kmh
❷ gear

CURVA DO SOL 130/209 ❶
DESCIDA DO SOL 85/138 ❷
RETA OPOSTA
'S' DO SENNA 55/89 ❷
SUBIDA DO LAGO 78/125 ❸
FERRA DURA
PINEIRINHO 60/97 ❷
MERGULHO 118/190 ❸
LARANJA
JUNCAO
ARQUEBAN CADA BICO DE PATO 45/72 ❶
SUBIDA DOS BOXES 160/258 ❻

RACE CLASSIFICATION

Pos	Driver	Nat	Car	Laps	Time
1	David Coulthard	GB	McLaren MP4-16-Mercedes V10	71	1h39m00.834s
2	Michael Schumacher	D	Ferrari F2001-Ferrari V10	71	+16.164s
3	Nick Heidfeld	D	Sauber C20-Petronas V10		+1 lap
4	Olivier Panis	F	BAR 003-Honda V10		+1 lap
5	Jarno Trulli	I	Jordan EJ11-Honda V10		+1 lap
6	Giancarlo Fisichella	I	Benetton B201-Renault V10		+1 lap
7	Jacques Villeneuve	CDN	BAR 003-Honda V10		+1 lap
8	Jean Alesi	F	Prost AP04-Acer V10		+1 lap
9	Tarso Marques	BR	Minardi PS01-European V10		+3 laps
10	Jenson Button	GB	Benetton B201-Renault V10		+7 laps
11	Heinz-Harald Frentzen	D	Jordan EJ11-Honda V10		+8 laps

Retirements		Nat	Car	Laps	Reason
Kimi Raikkonen		FIN	Sauber C20-Petronas V10	55	spin / tyre lost
Gaston Mazzacane		RA	Prost AP04-Acer V10	54	clutch
Ralf Schumacher		D	Williams FW23-BMW V10	54	spin
Eddie Irvine		GB	Jaguar R2-Ford Cosworth V10	52	spin / stalled
Juan Pablo Montoya		CO	Williams FW23-BMW V10	38	accident
Jos Verstappen		NL	Arrows A22-Asiatech V10	37	accident
Luciano Burti		BR	Jaguar R2-Ford Cosworth V10	30	water seal
Fernando Alonso		E	Minardi PS01-European V10	25	throttle
Enrique Bernoldi		BR	Arrows A22-Asiatech V10	15	hydraulics / gearbox
Rubens Barrichello		BR	Ferrari F2001-Ferrari V10	2	accident
Mika Hakkinen		FIN	McLaren MP4-16-Mercedes V10	0	hydraulics / clutch

FASTEST LAP   R Schumacher 1m15.693s lap 38 (127.343mph / 204.938kmh)

DRIVERS' CHAMPIONSHIP

1	Michael Schumacher	26
2	David Coulthard	20
3	Rubens Barrichello	10
4	Nick Heidfeld	7
5	Heinz-Harald Frentzen	5
6	Olivier Panis	3
7	Ralf Schumacher	2
	Jarno Trulli	2
9	Kimi Raikkonen	1
	Mika Hakkinen	1
	Giancarlo Fisichella	1

CONSTRUCTORS' CHAMPIONSHIP

1	Ferrari	36
2	McLaren-Mercedes	21
3	Sauber-Petronas	8
4	Jordan-Honda	7
5	BAR-Honda	3
6	Williams-BMW	2
7	Benetton-Renault	1

LAD OF HYPE AND GLORY

IN 2001 JUAN PABLO MONTOYA BECAME ONLY THE SEVENTH DRIVER TO WIN DURING HIS ROOKIE F1 SEASON. HE ALSO OVERTOOK SCHUEY SNR THREE TIMES WITHOUT THE COMPLIMENT BEING RETURNED. NOT A BAD START, ALL IN ALL

IT WAS A TYPICAL JUAN PABLO Montoya move. Quick. Decisive. Successful. Unfortunately, however, it got him into rather more trouble than almost anything he had done on track all season.

It was late in the season, on Friday morning at Indianapolis, where two years earlier he had won over the American public with a dominant performance in the nation's most famous race, the Indy 500.

Working his way towards the circuit's core via one of the labyrinthine feeder roads, the impetuous Colombian got bored traipsing along behind a driver who didn't appear to know where he was going. So he did what comes naturally and accelerated past. . . and that went against the local protocol. At Indy, you heed the instructions of an army of helpers dressed in fluorescent yellow jackets. Unamused, one such leapt out in front of Montoya and began banging on his bonnet and yelling about traffic regulations. Juan Pablo did much as he does when Michael Schumacher or any other of his F1 peers rails at him: he ignored the tirade and drove off. The marshal resorted to the only remaining tactic: abuse. "Bloody foreigners," he yelled at the fast-departing hire car.

Predictably, Montoya thought the incident quite funny. "The guy didn't have a clue who I was," he said, laughing. "I'm sure those guys in yellow are really nice people, but if you give them a bit of power they go a bit mad. I'm used to it, though. Remember, with qualifying and everything for the Indy 500 I spent three weeks here in 1999. . ." With that he rolled his eyes upwards and moved on to topics anew.

If any driver in the field of 22 was going to have a row with a marshal, you didn't need telling which it would be. The Indy incident was a cameo that encapsulated Montoya's maiden F1 season, both on and off the track. Getting under people's skin became something of a speciality.

From the moment he began testing with Williams in earnest, pre-season, there was talk of friction between the Colombian and his new team-mate Ralf Schumacher. "I don't suppose," team boss Frank Williams admitted, "that they are going to get along marvellously."

But why should they? At this level, self-centredness is a vital part of a racing driver's make-up, leastways if you are going to be a winner. In-fighting is fine, so long as it helps drive the team forward. Schuey Jnr unquestionably upped his game in 2001 – but with Montoya coming in he knew he didn't have much choice. Already, the previous season, Ralf had been shown up from time to time by rookie team-mate Jenson Button – but Montoya was an upstart with a difference: he was a vastly experienced newcomer, with the FIA Formula 3000 and Champ Car titles under his belt, as well as that Indy 500 win.

For the first half of the season, Ralf generally had the upper hand, although there were exceptions, such as Brazil and Austria. From France onwards, however, there was a gradual sea-change. Montoya began to make fewer mistakes and started to look the more convincing of two exceptionally good racers. Twice, at Magny-Cours and Silverstone, the team asked Ralf to move over for Juan Pablo, who was closing and, thanks to a different strategy, running faster. Twice Schuey Jnr claimed he had radio communication problems and failed to respond. Under his

LONG BEACH BOY:
Montoya broke all
records during his
maiden Champ Car
season in 1999 (below).
Experience gleaned in
the States helped him
fine-tune his racecraft
before he made what
many felt was an
overdue switch to F1

skin? Judge for yourself.

It had taken only until Brazil, race three, for Montoya to lay a marker with the elder Schumacher. Few drivers would have considered risking a punt in a gap that size against any rival, let alone the famously uncompromising defending champ. But Montoya had become accustomed to racing on ovals at 200mph or more. Threading his way through densely-packed traffic at that speed was second nature. To him alone, the space to Schuey's left at Interlagos probably looked huge. During the season, he tackled Schuey four times on track – and never lost (although Austria was probably a score draw, because they

both wound up in the gravel).

His first victory might have taken until Monza, but that was long overdue. By then, he should also have been basking in the reflected glory of wins at Interlagos and Hockenheim, at least.

After Montoya's maiden success in the Italian GP, a Williams employee mischievously pinned a sketch to the office wall. It showed three matchstick men on a podium. The first two, representing Montoya and Rubens Barrichello, had big smiles on their faces; the third, Ralf, bore a huge scowl. It was crude, but it captured the essence of the post-race body language.

The following weekend, a familiar figure (clue: stocky, smiling, Colombian passport) was reportedly handing out photocopies to friends in the paddock when the US-based Champ Car series visited Rockingham Motor Speedway in the UK.

While many of his peers steer clear of the media, Montoya – who used to be famously inept in front of a microphone, garrulous though he tended to be elsewhere – was a gracious and plain-speaking host throughout the campaign. His briefings were always well attended and they were seldom dull.

"Everyone keeps asking me about my home in Colombia as though it is some sort of mad country," he said at mid-season. "But what about England? You set fire to cows. That's mad . . ."

Montoya's was by no means a perfect season – but he learned by most of the mistakes he made and became a canny racer. Whereas at the start of the season he might overdrive if his tyres weren't up

to peak operating temperature (Austria, for instance), by the end he had learned the art of patience. He would bide his time and wait until the Michelins hit their sweet spot before mounting an assault (America was typical).

At one point Frank Williams was asked what differences there were between Montoya and Jenson Button, who had been discarded to make way for Colombia's most famous sportsman.

"Last year," Williams said, "Jenson would sit in the corner and listen, waiting for us to tell him what to do. It was all very new to him and he needed to build up his confidence as the year went on. Juan Pablo, I can assure you, came here with no self-doubts whatsoever." ■

CANADA DRAY: Things didn't always go well in F1 – and Montreal (main shot) was probably the nadir. Insets, below from left: a winner in British F3, 1996; Montoya lapped the field at Pau in 1998, when he became the only driver ever to have won the F3000 street race twice; with girlfriend Connie; on the grid at Monza, less than two hours away from his first grand prix victory

"JUAN PABLO, I CAN ASSURE YOU, CAME HERE WITH NO SELF-DOUBTS WHATSOEVER" FRANK WILLIAMS

PREMIO WARSTEINER DI SAN MARINO

SCHUMACHER WINS. NOT NORMALLY AN EYE-CATCHING HEADLINE, FRANKLY. BUT IT WAS ON THIS OCCASION

RALF MAN, RALF BISCUIT: Williams team members applaud the end of a long drought (main shot); Schuey Jnr won a very posh fruit salad bowl for his efforts (right)

AT THE START OF THE SEASON BMW MOTORSPORT boss Dr Mario Theissen smiled coyly whenever you broached the subject of his company winning races in 2001.

"We believe we will be ready to win next year," he would say. "This season? Well, perhaps if there is a problem with the red or silver cars it might happen, but we don't expect it."

It took all of four races to prove that this was a pile of tosh.

There wasn't much different about the Williams-BMW at Imola (other than a Keep Your Distance motif on the rear wing, a hangover of the team having been biffed up the rear four times in the opening three races). Its speed had been evident since Melbourne – especially in Brazil – and it remained so in the opening European race of the campaign. The McLarens of David Coulthard and Mika Hakkinen might have locked out the front row, but Ralf Schumacher took third and elbowed his elder brother out of the post-qualifying press conference (sorry Schumacher major, top three only) for the first time since last season's Belgian GP, nine races ago. Michael took a punt on running Bridgestone's harder tyre in the belief it would give him an edge in the race, but it didn't help in qualifying and nor would he have much luck later.

The outcome was effectively settled in the sprint to the Tamburello chicane. Coulthard didn't make a bad start, but his Mercedes V10 was something of a pantomime horse alongside Schuey Jnr's BMW thoroughbred. The Scot left just about enough room to his left to accommodate a Williams FW23, assuming the latter's driver was able to position it accurately to within a thousandth of a millimetre. And Ralf was.

THE GERMAN DROVE FAULTLESSLY TO NOTCH UP HIS MAIDEN GP WIN – AND HIS TEAM'S FIRST SINCE THE LUXEMBOURG GP ON SEPTEMBER 28 1997

"It was close," Coulthard said, "but I knew he was there. I was just a bit surprised at how quickly he was going in the opening stages. I thought he must be on a five-stop strategy or something."

As he trailed along in the Williams's wake, however, it didn't take long for him to work out that he was in for a whole afternoon of chasing a Schumacher, albeit not the one he was accustomed to wrestling. His best hope was for Ralf to make an error, but there was no sign of that. The German drove faultlessly to notch up his maiden GP win – and his team's first since the Luxembourg GP at the Nürburgring on September 28 1997. Since returning to F1 BMW had taken just 21 races to register a victory and tyre supplier Michelin needed only four.

His elder brother had done a passable impression of Tigger on steroids when he scored his first F1 triumph at Spa in 1992, but Ralf – who ensured that the Schumachers were the first siblings to have tasted success in world championship grands prix – was somewhat calmer. "It's a great feeling," he said, straight afterwards, "but it hasn't really sunk in yet. I just hope it is the first of many."

Coulthard was happy enough to be second, because Schuey Snr – whom many assumed had all but wrapped up the title after

THRUST WILLIAMS: at the start (right), Schuey Jnr appeared to benefit from the kind of supplementary boost enjoyed by Professor Pat Pending in epic episodes of *Wacky Races*. Above, Raikkonen wonders whether anyone in the Sauber pit is going to believe him when he explains that he crashed because his steering wheel fell off...

IF MUSIC BE THE LOVE OF FOOD...

Tongue planted as firmly in his cheek as his foot had been on the throttle, David Coulthard grinned after qualifying fastest for the first time this season (above) – and ending Michael Schumacher's run of seven straight pole positions.

"I'd like to apologise to the Italian fans if I have disappointed them," he said. "I will try not to do it again."

Truth was, however, that the atmosphere was more subdued in 2001 than is traditionally the case. And it had nothing to do with Michael Schumacher's indifferent form in qualifying or the race.

It is a tradition that you must queue to get in at Imola, because the streets are packed with humanity rather than cars, but this was Easter weekend and the circuit was quieter than normal. Much quieter. On race morning, usually the busiest by far, access was an absolute breeze because many punters opted to go to church before they pitched up to watch the race.

By start time the place was close to full and once the race was run, even after a Ferrari defeat, the crowd invaded the track and began trying to filch souvenirs (bits of pit apparatus, wheels, fuel churns, McLaren MP4-16s, that sort of thing).

The customary Imola effervescence was absent, however. "Easter," one local said, by way of explanation, "is not a time for motor racing. It is a time for going to church and seeing your family. People return to their home towns, see their friends and families and eat huge meals."

Religion, it seems, is still the number one religion – and Ferrari is beaten into fourth place by football and food.

TRULLI – DEEPLY MADDENING: Italy's one-man traffic jam eventually finished fifth

SCHUEY PLUMMETED DOWN THE ORDER LIKE A THREE-WHEELED MINARDI. IT WAS THE FIRST TIME IN 11 RACES THAT HE HAD FAILED TO REGISTER A PODIUM FINISH

Malaysia – plummeted down the order like a three-wheeled Minardi in the opening stages. Never a factor, the German pitted after 23 laps with a flat front left tyre and retired soon afterwards because a loose brake caliper was errantly machining away a wheel rim, hence the puncture. It was the first time in 11 races that he had failed to register a podium finish – and his departure allowed Coulthard to draw level at the head of the points table.

By way of minor consolation for Ferrari's fans, some small Brazilian bloke whom they don't much care for (even though he's an absolute gent) drove spiritedly. Rubens Barrichello's one-stop strategy wasn't as efficient as the two favoured by the pace-setters, and certainly wasn't helped by the fact that Jarno Trulli's Jordan held a) third place and b) everybody up in the opening stages; but he made best use of it in the circumstances to finish on the podium, about 10 seconds behind Coulthard and just ahead of Mika Hakkinen, who never recovered from the time he lost behind Trulli at the start.

The Jordan driver was shuffled down the order after the first round of pit stops, but he and team-mate Heinz-Harald Frentzen both collected points by rounding off the top six.

While there was obvious joy on one side of the Williams garage, there was mild satisfaction on the other. Overtaking might have been a conspicuously rare commodity, but Juan Pablo Montoya pulled off two solid moves to remind everyone that the spirit he showed in Brazil was in rude health. He dived past Olivier Panis's BAR-Honda on lap one and later elbowed Trulli aside spectacularly through a chicane. Gearbox failure denied him what should have been a points finish, but at least he lasted long enough to make a refuelling stop for the first time in his F1 career. ■

PLAIN SEEKING

As a motor racing circuit, Imola is essentially crap – but you can forgive its wholesale absence of overtaking opportunities.

As a place to appreciate the art of a grand prix driver per se, it is up there with the best (along with Monaco, which also manages to be spectacular without permitting drivers actually to race). Imola might be littered with chicanes, but average lap speeds remain high and drivers have to monster the kerbs to extract a decent qualifying time, so the end result is good to watch.

The whole paddock savours the annual trip to the plains of Emilia-Romagna. The circuit lies on the edge of the town with which it shares its name – and once you drift away from the caramel-coloured buildings all you can see are lush hills, vineyards, vineyards and more vineyards. While wildlife suffers in Britain through the gradual desecration of the countryside, here it thrives.

This year it was cold enough to snow in the higher outskirts of the region on Saturday morning, but that served only to make it look even prettier.

There is no such thing as a bad restaurant in these parts – and you'll get a top-class, three-course meal for about £15-£20, including decent wine and several flagons of Signor Moretti's finest ale.

When Bernie Ecclestone introduces a new range of GPs within the next few years (Russia, Patagonia, Guatemala, wherever), Imola – it is rumoured – will be one of the first European races to face the axe.

What a waste that would be.

ACCESS RATING FOR BRITS *****
A short hop from Bologna and not too far from Milan (where you should use Linate airport, if possible, because Malpensa is bleedin' miles away on the wrong side of town). Worth going even if there's not a race on – and sometimes especially when there's not a race on.

STARTING GRID

Pos	Driver	Time
	4 Coulthard	1m23.054s
	3 Hakkinen	1m23.282s
	5 R Schumacher	1m23.357s
	1 M Schumacher	1m23.593s
	12 Trulli	1m23.658s
	2 Barrichello	1m23.786s
	6 Montoya	1m24.141s
	9 Panis	1m24.213s
	11 Frentzen	1m24.436s
	17 Raikkonen	1m24.671s
	10 Villeneuve	1m24.769s
	16 Heidfeld	1m25.007s
	18 Irvine	1m25.392s
	22 Alesi	1m25.411s
	19 Burti	1m25.572s
	15 Bernoldi	1m25.872s
	14 Verstappen	1m26.062s
	21 Alonso	1m26.855s
	7 Fisichella	1m26.902s
	23 Mazzacane	1m27.750s
	8 Button	1m27.758s
	20 Marques	1m28.281s

April 15 2001
AUTODROMO ENZO E DINO FERRARI, IMOLA
CIRCUIT LENGTH: 3.065miles / 4.933km

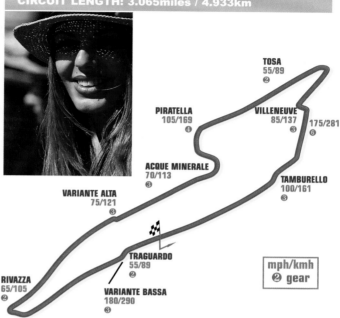

TOSA 55/89 ②
PIRATELLA 105/169 ①
VILLENEUVE 85/137 ③
175/281 ⑥
ACQUE MINERALE 70/113 ③
TAMBURELLO 100/161 ③
VARIANTE ALTA 75/121 ③
VARIANTE BASSA 180/290 ③
TRAGUARDO 55/89 ②
RIVAZZA 65/105 ②

mph/kmh
② gear

RACE CLASSIFICATION

Pos	Driver	Nat	Car	Laps	Time
1	Ralf Schumacher	D	Williams FW23-BMW V10	62	1h30m44.817s
2	David Coulthard	GB	McLaren MP4-16-Mercedes V10	62	+4.352s
3	Rubens Barrichello	BR	Ferrari F2001-Ferrari V10	62	+34.766s
4	Mika Hakkinen	FIN	McLaren MP4-16-Mercedes V10	62	+36.315s
5	Jarno Trulli	I	Jordan EJ11-Honda V10	62	+1m25.558s
6	Heinz-Harald Frentzen	D	Jordan EJ11-Honda V10		+1 lap
7	Nick Heidfeld	D	Sauber C20-Petronas V10		+1 lap
8	Olivier Panis	F	BAR 003-Honda V10		+1 lap
9	Jean Alesi	F	Prost AP04-Acer V10		+1 lap
10	Enrique Bernoldi	BR	Arrows A22-Asiatech V10		+2 laps
11	Luciano Burti	BR	Jaguar R2-Ford Cosworth V10		+2 laps
12	Jenson Button	GB	Benetton B201-Renault V10		+2 laps
Retirements		**Nat**	**Car**	**Laps**	**Reason**
	Tarso Marques	BR	Minardi PS01-European V10	50	fuel line
	Juan Pablo Montoya	CO	Williams FW23-BMW V10	48	gearbox
	Eddie Irvine	GB	Jaguar R2-Ford Cosworth V10	42	engine
	Giancarlo Fisichella	I	Benetton B201-Renault V10	31	engine misfire
	Jacques Villeneuve	CDN	BAR 003-Honda V10	30	engine
	Gaston Mazzacane	RA	Prost AP04-Acer V10	28	engine
	Michael Schumacher	D	Ferrari F2001-Ferrari V10	24	brake caliper/puncture
	Kimi Raikkonen	FIN	Sauber C20-Petronas V10	17	steering wheel / spin
	Jos Verstappen	NL	Arrows A22-Asiatech V10	6	exhaust
	Fernando Alonso	E	Minardi PS01-European V10	5	accident

FASTEST LAP R Schumacher 1m25.524s lap 27 (129.026mph / 207.647kmh)

DRIVERS' CHAMPIONSHIP

1	Michael Schumacher	26
	David Coulthard	26
3	Rubens Barrichello	14
4	Ralf Schumacher	12
5	Nick Heidfeld	7
6	Heinz-Harald Frentzen	6
7	Mika Hakkinen	4
	Jarno Trulli	4
9	Olivier Panis	3
10	Kimi Raikkonen	1
	Giancarlo Fisichella	1

CONSTRUCTORS' CHAMPIONSHIP

1	Ferrari	40
2	McLaren-Mercedes	30
3	Williams-BMW	12
4	Jordan-Honda	10
5	Sauber-Petronas	8
6	BAR-Honda	3
7	Benetton-Renault	1

GRAN PREMIO MARLBORO DE ESPAÑA

THEY SAY CHAMPIONS NEED LUCK AS WELL AS SKILL. FOR MICHAEL SCHUMACHER, RACES DON'T COME ANY LUCKIER THAN BARCELONA. MIKA HAKKINEN WAS THE MAN WHO SUFFERED

Spanish inquisition: Schuey wonders whether he'll be able to keep the fully-awake (for e) Hakkinen at bay as they lead the field through the first few turns. He couldn't... but it dn't matter because luck was on his side. Right, the Finn has earned enough from motor acing to subscribe to a super-fast recovery service that gets to you quicker than the AA

WAS BARCELONA PERHAPS THE ROOT CAUSE OF MIKA

Hakkinen's decision to take a break from racing? Michael Schumacher scored one of his most fortunate grand prix wins in Catalunya after the Finn's leading McLaren failed him on the final lap.

This was the one they had all been talking about. Spain. The return of legal electronic gizmos. The levelling of the playing field. What would happen to the established order?

Precisely nothing. Some had predicted that those grey-area inhabiting, envelope-pushing Italians would go backwards. But who sat on the pole? Schuey, of course. And which team had its worst qualifying performance of the season? Those whiter-than-white, good old English chaps at Williams. Not in the script, that. So let's forget all about innuendo and go motor racing. . .

Schumacher converted his pole position and established an early three-second lead over Hakkinen, which he retained at the first pit stop. Hakkinen ran five laps longer in the first stint but failed to make any headway. It looked like one of their classic battles à la Suzuka 2000, with both men pushing for all they were worth. When Schumacher made his second and final stop on lap

TOOTH PACED: Schuey leads a chorus of cheesy grins (above) as Montoya (left, and in action below) appears on the podium for the first time and Villeneuve (right) does so for the first time in BAR clobber

ON YOUR MARQUES: he started and finished last. . . but the picture is a paragon of colour, so Tarso (right) makes it in because the art editor prefers composition to subject

MIKA SEEMED HOME FREE FOR HIS FIRST WIN IN ALMOST NINE MONTHS, BUT THEN THE CLUTCH EXPLODED ON HIS LAST LAP

42 of the 65, however, Hakkinen went fully eight laps farther before emerging with a three-second lead. Mika seemed home free for his first win in almost nine months, but then the clutch exploded on his last lap.

Schumacher, sportingly, did not celebrate with his usual exuberance. When Mika came sadly back on the pod of David Coulthard's sister McLaren, Michael was the first over to him with a consoling arm.

"You don't like to win a race like that," Schuey admitted. "I was simply sorry because I think we had an entertaining race. He jumped me at the second pit stop and it reminded me of some of our battles last year. Seeing him retire with five corners to go was shocking because he had done everything right."

Schumacher had his own problems and had given up the chase.

"I had a huge vibration, most likely in the tyres. I was going slowly down the straights so as not to risk a delamination. We even thought about an extra pit stop but it got no worse, so I carried on slowly. It's a bit of a mystery because I had three sets of new tyres and they should have all been equal. I actually managed to pull away from Mika after the first stop and I expected it would work the same way again, but it wasn't like that."

Juan Pablo Montoya arrived in Spain as the only driver among

METTLE MIKA

Mika Hakkinen came to Spain determined to win. He needed to re-establish himself in the championship battle. Suspension failure in Melbourne, lacklustre sixth in Malaysia, clutch failure on the line at Interlagos, an apparently disinterested fourth at Imola. . . it did not look like the launch pad for a third world championship.

Schumacher and Ferrari took pole at the first three races but David Coulthard proved that a McLaren was still a worthy tool when he started at the head of the pack in San Marino. Now Mika wanted to stick it to Ferrari. He almost made it, but Michael pipped him to top spot by 0.08s.

No matter. The McLaren felt good in race trim and Mika was confident. It wasn't misplaced confidence either. In the McLaren pit, Erja Hakkinen's smile was almost as wide as Michael's car when Mika emerged from his second stop with what was clearly a winning advantage. But it soon turned to a gasp of despair as Mika slowed, the McLaren hobbled by an exploding clutch on the last lap.

Hakkinen himself looked shell-shocked. Leaving Barcelona, five races in, the score was: Michael 36, Mika 4. There are mountains to climb and there are mountains. This looked like Everest without oxygen.

A year earlier, Mika had been accused of a drop-off in motivation. His riposte had been perfect as he trounced everyone in Austria, pulled off that move in Belgium and headed into the final four races in front. But could he do it again? He had been 10 years in the F1 business, he had a wife and a new young son, Hugo. The bank balance was healthier than it would ever need to be. Who knew his true mental state?

Convention suggests it is hard for a racer to contemplate retirement, or even a sabbatical, when he has a winning car at his disposal. But, come September, we would know differently. Barcelona, you can bet, sowed the seeds.

BAR TENDING: Villeneuve receives a handy tip for the 3.45 at Haydock

JACQUES VILLENEUVE BENEFITED FROM HAKKINEN'S WOES TO RECORD HIS TEAM'S FIRST PODIUM FINISH

the 22 yet to record a race finish. He wanted to put that right. But 12th was not the ideal starting position and BMW was still not confident enough in the reliability of its traction control to run it for the race. There was nothing wrong with their launch control, however – Montoya was sixth after the first corner.

Tucked in behind Trulli's Jordan, Juan Pablo couldn't pass the Italian but leap-frogged him at the first stop. Schuey Jnr spun, Barrichello stopped with a suspension failure and when Montoya saw Hakkinen stop, too, he knew that his first F1 finish would bring him six points.

"I'm pleased about that," he beamed. "The first four races have been hard. I just kept pushing all day long. My car was a bit tricky to drive and the Ferraris and McLarens were in a different league this weekend."

Jacques Villeneuve, who was not using launch control because BAR didn't yet have sufficient faith in the system, also benefited from Hakkinen's woes to record his team's first podium finish.

"Everyone in the team has worked hard for the last three seasons and finally this is the boost they all needed." Jacques said. "The car was hard work, but it looks like it was difficult for everyone."

Slick work by BAR at the second pit stop allowed Villeneuve to pass Trulli's Jordan-Honda, but the Italian scored his third successive points finish and fourth place was his best result so far this year.

It simply wasn't McLaren's day. Coulthard, fourth on the grid, failed to get away on the formation lap and was obliged to start from the back. In the circumstances, scoring two points for fifth place was a bonus. Especially after he damaged the MP4-16's nose in the first-lap scramble and had to pit for a replacement.

Nick Heidfeld stayed in touch throughout and was rewarded with the final point after another creditable performance from Sauber. ■

TRIVIAL PURSUITS

If the authorities wanted to make Barcelona a more credible venue, they would chuck in a few surprises. Perhaps make drivers race anti-clockwise, plant a few saplings halfway down the main straight or set a few bulls loose on about lap four.

Trouble is, every team pounds round Barcelona for week after week during winter testing. The climate being a touch more favourable than Silverstone's, it makes perfect sense to do so. Shall we sit in a damp pit garage for a couple of days and stare into space, or get on with a bit of development work? Cue a ticket to Spain.

As a corollary, however, by the time they pitch up to race the cars more or less know the way around the track on their own. Free practice on Friday is quiet compared to circuits where teams don't get to test at all, such as Monaco and Canada. Chassis are perfectly fine-tuned when they arrive, drivers qualify, race in the order that they started (more or less) and go home. If it stays dry, the race will be dull. If it rains Michael Schumacher will win by at least half a minute. And it will probably still be dull.

For all the negative aspects, however, Barcelona has its good points. The city, half an hour from the track by road, is one of Europe's finest (but keep you wallet tucked away safely). Tickets, beer and food are cheap, and the race is never a sell-out because the locals much prefer racing on two wheels to four. Post-race traffic jams are not unknown, but they disperse swiftly.

ACCESS RATING FOR BRITS ★★★★
Things have become much easier in the past couple of years, after they finally got round to putting up some signposts at the airport. Follow A7 Francia/Girona. It shouldn't take long, although there's usually at least one upturned lorry en route

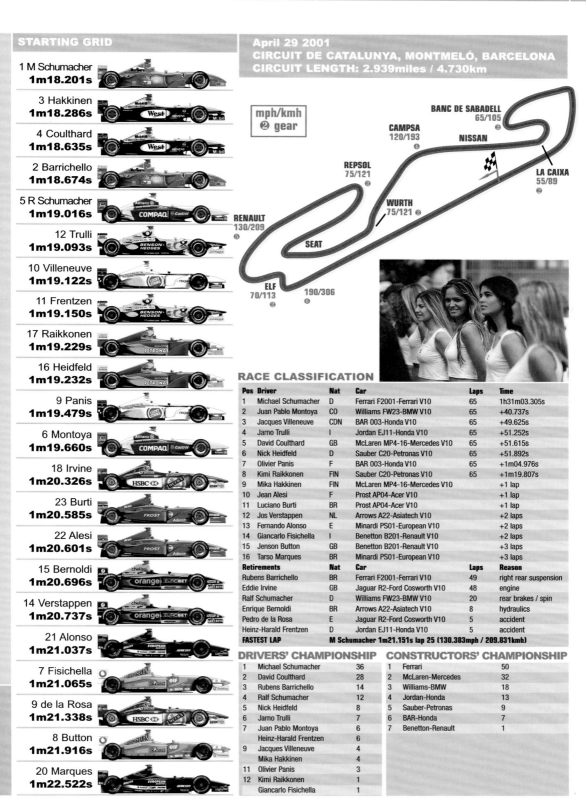

STARTING GRID

1 M Schumacher **1m18.201s**

3 Hakkinen **1m18.286s**

4 Coulthard **1m18.635s**

2 Barrichello **1m18.674s**

5 R Schumacher **1m19.016s**

12 Trulli **1m19.093s**

10 Villeneuve **1m19.122s**

11 Frentzen **1m19.150s**

17 Raikkonen **1m19.229s**

16 Heidfeld **1m19.232s**

9 Panis **1m19.479s**

6 Montoya **1m19.660s**

18 Irvine **1m20.326s**

23 Burti **1m20.585s**

22 Alesi **1m20.601s**

15 Bernoldi **1m20.696s**

14 Verstappen **1m20.737s**

21 Alonso **1m21.037s**

7 Fisichella **1m21.065s**

9 de la Rosa **1m21.338s**

8 Button **1m21.916s**

20 Marques **1m22.522s**

April 29 2001
CIRCUIT DE CATALUNYA, MONTMELÓ, BARCELONA
CIRCUIT LENGTH: 2.939miles / 4.730km

mph/kmh
❷ gear

BANC DE SABADELL 65/105 ❷

CAMPSA 120/193 ❹

NISSAN

REPSOL 75/121 ❷

LA CAIXA 55/89 ❷

WURTH 75/121 ❷

RENAULT 130/209 ❺

SEAT

ELF 70/113 ❼   190/306 ❻

RACE CLASSIFICATION

Pos	Driver	Nat	Car	Laps	Time
1	Michael Schumacher	D	Ferrari F2001-Ferrari V10	65	1h31m03.305s
2	Juan Pablo Montoya	CO	Williams FW23-BMW V10	65	+40.737s
3	Jacques Villeneuve	CDN	BAR 003-Honda V10	65	+49.625s
4	Jarno Trulli	I	Jordan EJ11-Honda V10	65	+51.252s
5	David Coulthard	GB	McLaren MP4-16-Mercedes V10	65	+51.615s
6	Nick Heidfeld	D	Sauber C20-Petronas V10	65	+51.892s
7	Olivier Panis	F	BAR 003-Honda V10	65	+1m04.976s
8	Kimi Raikkonen	FIN	Sauber C20-Petronas V10	65	+1m19.807s
9	Mika Hakkinen	FIN	McLaren MP4-16-Mercedes V10		+1 lap
10	Jean Alesi	F	Prost AP04-Acer V10		+1 lap
11	Luciano Burti	BR	Prost AP04-Acer V10		+1 lap
12	Jos Verstappen	NL	Arrows A22-Asiatech V10		+2 laps
13	Fernando Alonso	E	Minardi PS01-European V10		+2 laps
14	Giancarlo Fisichella	I	Benetton B201-Renault V10		+2 laps
15	Jenson Button	GB	Benetton B201-Renault V10		+3 laps
16	Tarso Marques	BR	Minardi PS01-European V10		+3 laps

Retirements	Nat	Car	Laps	Reason
Rubens Barrichello	BR	Ferrari F2001-Ferrari V10	49	right rear suspension
Eddie Irvine	GB	Jaguar R2-Ford Cosworth V10	48	engine
Ralf Schumacher	D	Williams FW23-BMW V10	20	rear brakes / spin
Enrique Bernoldi	BR	Arrows A22-Asiatech V10	8	hydraulics
Pedro de la Rosa	E	Jaguar R2-Ford Cosworth V10	5	accident
Heinz-Harald Frentzen	D	Jordan EJ11-Honda V10	5	accident

FASTEST LAP   M Schumacher 1m21.151s lap 25 (130.383mph / 209.831kmh)

DRIVERS' CHAMPIONSHIP

1	Michael Schumacher	36
2	David Coulthard	28
3	Rubens Barrichello	14
4	Ralf Schumacher	12
5	Nick Heidfeld	8
6	Jarno Trulli	7
7	Juan Pablo Montoya	6
	Heinz-Harald Frentzen	6
9	Jacques Villeneuve	4
	Mika Hakkinen	4
11	Olivier Panis	3
12	Kimi Raikkonen	1
	Giancarlo Fisichella	1

CONSTRUCTORS' CHAMPIONSHIP

1	Ferrari	50
2	McLaren-Mercedes	32
3	Williams-BMW	18
4	Jordan-Honda	13
5	Sauber-Petronas	9
6	BAR-Honda	7
7	Benetton-Renault	1

GROSSER A1 PREIS VON ÖSTERREICH

THE CHANCES OF WINNING A MODERN-DAY GRAND PRIX FROM THE FOURTH ROW ARE SLIMMER THAN MOST OF DAVID COULTHARD'S GIRLFRIENDS. THAT'S WHY THE SCOT WAS MORE THAN SATISFIED WITH A JOB WELL DONE IN AUSTRIA

SCOTLAND THE RAVE: Coulthard celebrates after underlining his championship credentials (for at least the next five minutes, anyway). Inset, DC plays charades. Two words... no, it's not a sport. . . team orders? Very good Michael, well done

BLUE STREET HILLS: the scenery in Austria is gorgeous, or at least it would be if all those bloody photographers weren't in the way. Bottom, from left: Montoya plays the hard man a bit too successfully and takes himself off as well as Schuey. Kimi Raikkonen and a tuft of grass. Schuey lines up Panis while working his way back through the field

AFTER WARM-UP ON SUNDAY MORNING DAVID COULTHARD gave a smile and a shrug of resignation. Mika Hakkinen was quickest, David second. The balance was perfect, hence the grin. But he was starting from row four, hence the resignation.

But if this was the most sophisticated sport in the world, then try explaining to Billy Punter why four cars remained rooted to the spot when the lights changed. Launch control? Something of a misnomer. . .

Hakkinen went nowhere, hammering a final nail into the coffin that bore Mika's lingering hopes of mounting a championship challenge. More interestingly for Coulthard, Trulli's Jordan and Heidfeld's Sauber also failed to get away. David was up to fifth when the Safety Car was despatched to allow the mayhem on the grid to be sorted out. And, better than that, both Williams-BMWs got around Schumacher's pole position Ferrari. From seventh, Coulthard had gone for a heavy fuel load, hoping to be able to stay in touch and then exploit what he anticipated would be a longer range than the Ferraris.

At the front, Schuey Jnr's challenge was over after 10 laps when the Williams was sidelined with a braking problem and it was left to Montoya to fend off the Ferrari challenge (plus that of a flying Jos Verstappen, whose Arrows was thus a light, two-stop fuel load and was running improbably close to the front). The characteristics of the Michelin tyre here meant that Montoya was quick initially, then slowed in comparison to the Bridgestone-shod

HAKKINEN WENT NOWHERE, HAMMERING A FINAL NAIL INTO THE COFFIN THAT BORE MIKA'S LINGERING HOPES OF MOUNTING A CHAMPIONSHIP CHALLENGE

cars, then was fully competitive again by the end of the stint as the grooves wore down and the rubber came back in.

Schumacher was soon anxious to pass and Montoya, predictably, mounted a spirited defence. When Michael tried to go around the outside of the Colombian into Turn Two, Juan Pablo braked late and very deep – but too deep. He slid off and took the Ferrari with him. Montoya resumed across the gravel and the Ferrari scrabbled back from the marbles, but not before Rubens Barrichello, Verstappen, Coulthard, Kimi Raikkonen and Olivier Panis had gone by. Montoya was rewarded with a clenched fist salute from Schumacher, but for all that Michael didn't like it, Coulthard was deeply grateful. When Verstappen pitted early for his first stop, only Barrichello remained in front of the Scot's McLaren. Schumacher, meanwhile, got his head down and quickly repassed Raikkonen and Panis.

With the A1-Ring being a one-stop race for anyone not driving an Arrows, pit performance was obviously going to be crucial. With light fuel/used tyres generally being quicker than new rubber/heavy fuel, he who went longest would win. Unless, of

FIRST AMONG SEQUELS

The first viewing came at Interlagos, the sequel at the A1-Ring.

In Brazil, Montoya made it quite clear that he was not going to allow Michael Schumacher to drive around the outside of him into Turn One. Not even with a light Ferrari on a two-stop fuel load while Juan himself carried half a race's worth.

The next tussle came in Austria – and this time you could understand Schumacher's frustration. Montoya's Michelins were going through a trough and Michael's Bridgestone-shod Ferrari was much quicker. On the run up to Turn Two, in spite of his rival's BMW grunt, Michael was alongside. But turning in was another matter. Michael was very late on the brakes, Juan even later. The Williams had no chance of making the corner and, of course, it didn't. Off they both went, losing places. But never mind that. Montoya had underlined his point – you might be Michael Schumacher, but you can't take liberties with me.

"I was a little upset obviously because there was no way he could make the corner and all he was trying to do was take me with him," Schumacher said in the immediate aftermath. "I'll have a word with him about it."

Before he did though, he had a look at the video and thought better of it. Okay, Montoya had gone too deep but, he, Michael, had compromised himself when he might have known what was coming. One to swallow and file away in the memory bank.

Rubens Barrichello's annoyance at having to move over for Schumacher was harder to fathom. He was only ahead of Michael because of the Montoya incident and, over the season, it wasn't hard to see where Ferrari's championship challenge was coming from. McLaren and Ron Dennis might not have liked it, but the time for Rubens (with Ferrari's Jean Todt) to get the hump about moving out of Michael's way is the weekend he outqualifies and outraces him.

MARKETABLE GARDENER: former champ Villeneuve kicks up the dust

COULTHARD DROVE A SUPERB OUT LAP. THE CARDS HAD FALLEN FOR HIM, BUT HE TOOK HIS CHANCE AND DROVE BRILLIANTLY

course, Ferrari brought Schumacher in first and asked Barrichello to slow Coulthard.

It looked like that might be Ferrari's ploy when Michael arrived first. In reality though, he had simply used more fuel than Rubens. Michael brakes with his left foot, which is not as fuel efficient, while Rubens is one of only four drivers who still uses his right. Coulthard is another. When Michael had an off at Turn Three on his out lap, it looked to be a straight fight; David versus Rubens. With sufficient juice to go an extra couple of laps, Coulthard turned in the fastest lap of the afternoon and then drove a superb out lap. He was ahead. The cards had fallen for him, but he took his chance and drove brilliantly.

In the closing stages the leading trio closed up. Schumacher, at the back, was the quickest man on the track. And Barrichello could not get close enough to Coulthard to launch a meaningful challenge. To compound his misery, Ferrari "sporting" director Jean Todt came onto the radio and ordered Rubens to cede second place to Michael. The Brazilian had to be told (sorry, asked) more than once, but finally he moved over out of the final turn. He had made his point.

There was no champagne on the podium. The previous evening, McLaren-Mercedes had been stunned by the news that Paul Morgan, co-founder of Ilmor (which designs and builds the team's V10s) had died when he crashed his historic plane, a World War II Sea Fury.

Raikkonen was a superb fourth for Sauber, despite a problem with his left rear wheel in the pits. Panis finished fifth for BAR and Verstappen earned a much-deserved point after his spirited afternoon.

Coulthard denied that Hakkinen's first-lap retirement meant that McLaren would now concentrate on him, but Schumacher spelt it out. "It is pretty obvious who McLaren will back for the championship," he said. "I think Mika is too far away now." ∎

DEAD PETS SOCIETY

The terrain is straight from The Sound of Music. The A1-Ring nestles in the Styrian foothills, although the lushness of the surrounding greenery tells you that the area is exposed to a fair bit of rain.

It is perhaps the most pastoral of all F1 settings – and certainly the only one where you can see cows grazing in the background, apparently indifferent to F1 cars blazing past no more than a couple of fields away.

Glance along any one of the valleys that are visible from the track and you might well see a golden eagle soaring high, on the lookout for a mouse-sized snack.

On top of its natural magnificence, the A1-Ring also promotes good racing: slow corner leading into long straight followed by slow corner equals passing opportunities. The track has been damned in the past, largely because it is a poor shadow of the old, ultra-fast Österreichring that once occupied parts of the same site. But while the high-speed spectacle of yore has gone, at least some kind of spectacle remains.

And now for the bad news. . .

There is very little in the way of infrastructure, so many people stay in local guesthouses that have a common characteristic: wooden floors strewn with animal pelts. And if there's no room left on the floor, they drape them all over walls and banister rails. Which is fine if you like that sort of thing.

The cows adjacent to the racetrack are just about the only living creatures you will see (apart from the eagles, which are mercifully out of shooting range).

ACCESS RATING FOR BRITS *

A total pain. At least two hours from any airport of consequence (or one from Graz, although private jet owners can park almost opposite, at the Zeltweg military airbase). For the really adventurous, Calais is about 15 hours by car.

STARTING GRID

Pos	Driver	Time
1	M Schumacher	1m9.562s
6	Montoya	1m9.686s
5	R Schumacher	1m9.769s
2	Barrichello	1m9.786s
12	Trulli	1m10.202s
16	Heidfeld	1m10.211s
4	Coulthard	1m10.331s
3	Hakkinen	1m10.342s
17	Raikkonen	1m10.396s
9	Panis	1m10.435s
11	Frentzen	1m10.923s
10	Villeneuve	1m11.058s
18	Irvine	1m11.632s
19	de la Rosa	1m11.752s
15	Bernoldi	1m11.823s
14	Verstappen	1m12.187s
23	Burti	1m12.206s
21	Alonso	1m12.640s
7	Fisichella	1m12.644s
22	Alesi	1m 12.910s
8	Button	1m13.459s
20	Marques	1m13.585s

May 13 2001
A1-RING, SPIELBERG
CIRCUIT LENGTH: 2.688miles / 4.326km

REMUS KURVE 40/64 ❶

175/282 ❻

NIKI LAUDA KURVE 100/161 ❶

175/282 ❻

145/233 ❶

GÖSSER KURVE 60/97 ❷

POWER HORSE KURVE 110/177 ❶

JOCHEN RINDT KURVE 115/185 ❶

170/274 ❻

mph/kmh ❷ gear

CASTROL KURVE 75/121 ❷

MOBILKOM KURVE 90/145 ❸

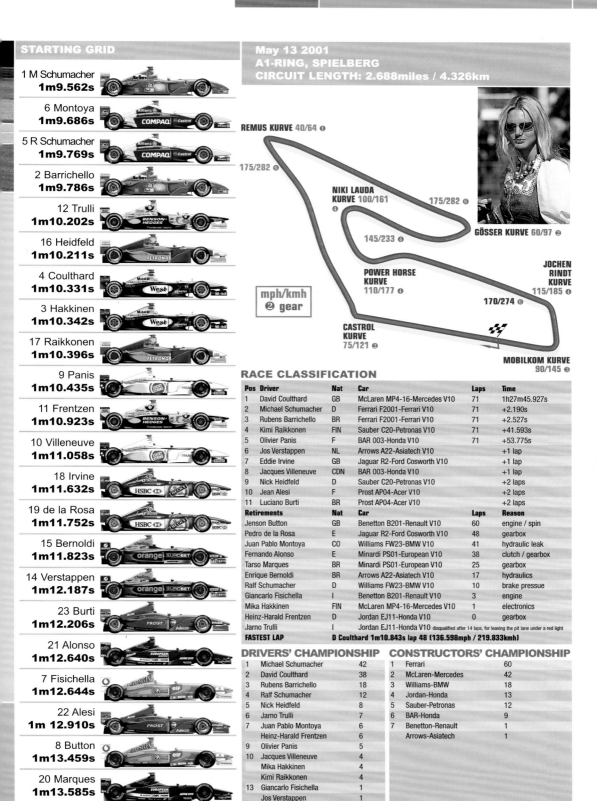

RACE CLASSIFICATION

Pos	Driver	Nat	Car	Laps	Time
1	David Coulthard	GB	McLaren MP4-16-Mercedes V10	71	1h27m45.927s
2	Michael Schumacher	D	Ferrari F2001-Ferrari V10	71	+2.190s
3	Rubens Barrichello	BR	Ferrari F2001-Ferrari V10	71	+2.527s
4	Kimi Raikkonen	FIN	Sauber C20-Petronas V10	71	+41.593s
5	Olivier Panis	F	BAR 003-Honda V10	71	+53.775s
6	Jos Verstappen	NL	Arrows A22-Asiatech V10		+1 lap
7	Eddie Irvine	GB	Jaguar R2-Ford Cosworth V10		+1 lap
8	Jacques Villeneuve	CDN	BAR 003-Honda V10		+1 lap
9	Nick Heidfeld	D	Sauber C20-Petronas V10		+2 laps
10	Jean Alesi	F	Prost AP04-Acer V10		+2 laps
11	Luciano Burti	BR	Prost AP04-Acer V10		+2 laps

Retirements	Nat	Car	Laps	Reason
Jenson Button	GB	Benetton B201-Renault V10	60	engine / spin
Pedro de la Rosa	E	Jaguar R2-Ford Cosworth V10	48	gearbox
Juan Pablo Montoya	CO	Williams FW23-BMW V10	41	hydraulic leak
Fernando Alonso	E	Minardi PS01-European V10	38	clutch / gearbox
Tarso Marques	BR	Minardi PS01-European V10	25	gearbox
Enrique Bernoldi	BR	Arrows A22-Asiatech V10	17	hydraulics
Ralf Schumacher	D	Williams FW23-BMW V10	10	brake pressue
Giancarlo Fisichella	I	Benetton B201-Renault V10	3	engine
Mika Hakkinen	FIN	McLaren MP4-16-Mercedes V10	1	electronics
Heinz-Harald Frentzen	D	Jordan EJ11-Honda V10	0	gearbox
Jarno Trulli	I	Jordan EJ11-Honda V10 disqualified after 14 laps, for leaving the pit lane under a red light		

FASTEST LAP D Coulthard 1m10.843s lap 48 (136.598mph / 219.833kmh)

DRIVERS' CHAMPIONSHIP

1	Michael Schumacher	42
2	David Coulthard	38
3	Rubens Barrichello	18
4	Ralf Schumacher	12
5	Nick Heidfeld	8
6	Jarno Trulli	7
7	Juan Pablo Montoya	6
	Heinz-Harald Frentzen	6
9	Olivier Panis	5
10	Jacques Villeneuve	4
	Mika Hakkinen	4
	Kimi Raikkonen	4
13	Giancarlo Fisichella	1
	Jos Verstappen	1

CONSTRUCTORS' CHAMPIONSHIP

1	Ferrari	60
2	McLaren-Mercedes	42
3	Williams-BMW	18
4	Jordan-Honda	13
5	Sauber-Petronas	12
6	BAR-Honda	9
7	Benetton-Renault	1
	Arrows-Asiatech	1

GRAND PRIX DE MONACO

DAVID COULTHARD TOOK A SUPERB POLE POSITION BUT WAS LAPPED BY MICHAEL SCHUMACHER INSIDE 30 LAPS. HOW? IT HAD SOMETHING TO DO WITH A BRAZILIAN IN, ER, AN ARROWS

HERR RAISING: Ferrari's mechanics laud their somewhat spawny talisman (right). Left, Bernoldi and Coulthard offer conclusive proof that Monaco is not a racing circuit, as such

THERE IS MURPHY'S LAW, SOD'S LAW AND then there is what happened to David Coulthard in Monte Carlo. In the words of Ron Dennis: "Anyone who outqualifies Michael Schumacher and Mika Hakkinen around Monte Carlo can justifiably feel very proud of himself."

Coulthard did. Hakkinen stopped the clock in 1m17.74s, Schumacher in 1m 17.63s and Coulthard in 1m17.43s. Two tenths. Not a lot, you might think. But two tenths quicker than Schumacher around the principality is a big deal. Believe it.

And then what happened? For the second time in three races DC could not get the McLaren off the line. Despite Dennis alluding to countless trouble-free launch control starts in testing, the McLaren would not leave the dummy grid. Again the Scot would start from the back. Heartbreaking.

Hakkinen fared little better. After 15 laps he felt his car pulling to the right and pitted. There was one more exploratory lap before he called it a day.

And so Schumacher scored an untroubled fifth win around the famous streets, equalling Graham Hill's achievement and bringing himself to within one victory of Ayrton Senna's all-time record of six in Monaco. As a race it was as compelling a spectacle as drying paint. But even that has a better finish.

"Although it looked easy it was still hard," Schumacher claimed. "People say it's easier with traction control but you actually go faster, which is harder."

Juan Pablo Montoya was mighty here in Formula 3000 and there were many anticipating fireworks on his first visit as a grand prix driver. His Williams team-mate Ralf Schumacher is not sucked in by the romance of Monaco. He thinks it is both Mickey Mouse and dangerous at the same time. The smart money, therefore, was on Juan Pablo being the

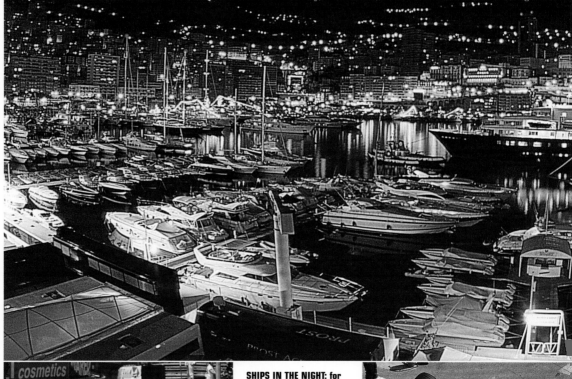

SHIPS IN THE NIGHT: for all that Monaco is a poor excuse for a racetrack, there are valid reasons (above) to go there. Left, Jacques Villeneuve put his poor form in the principality behind him and finished fourth

Williams pace-setter. Wrong. Ralf was fifth, and best of the rest, while Montoya was two slots further back and almost three-quarters of a second slower. In the race, JPM threw it into the wall at the swimming pool complex on lap three and Ralf fell foul of a hydraulics problem with 20 laps to go. Not one to remember, all in all.

This opened the way for Eddie Irvine to record Jaguar's first podium finish in F1. The team had major new aerodynamic developments courtesy of technical whizz Mark Handford, with a new floor, diffuser, rear crash structure and wing. And there was plenty of input from the driver too. Irvine is always a factor in Monaco, quick and mistake-free.

Jacques Villeneuve, not renowned for his local expertise here, chased Irvine hard and scored a good fourth place for BAR. Which brings us back to DC. . .

AS A RACE IT WAS AS COMPELLING A SPECTACLE AS DRYING PAINT. BUT EVEN THAT HAS A BETTER FINISH

WINGDINGS: Heinz-Harald Frentzen marmalised his Jordan (left) after turning about 200 metres too soon while going through the tunnel. The team tried out aesthetically crap wings (right) until the FIA barred them

MENACE THE DENNIS

"Why do you say you can't overtake at Monte Carlo?"

Following the Coulthard/Bernoldi debacle, the question was posed to McLaren boss Ron Dennis a fortnight later in Canada. He might have dismissed it as the enquiry of a journalist who normally covered tiddlywinks had it not come from Thierry Tassin, a respected former racer.

"If the guy ahead is obstructive then, without risking the car, it's not on," Dennis replied.

"But Jos Verstappen managed to pass five people," Tassin countered.

How had the Dutchman done it?

"The Arrows is quick in a straight line, which obviously helps, but you still have to be able to take advantage," Verstappen said. "Some people were having a confidence lift through the tunnel but I stayed flat out. That gave me an opportunity under braking for the harbour chicane and I passed three cars there. Jenson Button was tougher. He braked very late into it as well, so we went two abreast around it and I outbraked him into the next corner. I enjoyed that.

"The secret is planning and maybe taking a bit more risk. In Austria, for example, everybody went for the inside at Turn One, braked and queued up. I went to the left, braked much later and passed three or four people. That's nothing to do with fuel load. It's about reflexes and being prepared to go for it. Some drivers are a bit cautious at the start and the first lap gives you most opportunities, especially the first three corners.

"Some people are easier than others, for sure, and every time is different. Sometimes a guy you passed easily the race before has a better car.

"The tough guys? Michael, of course, Ralf, Montoya and Jacques Villeneuve. The soft touches? I know, but I'm not saying. . ."

CAT TRICK: Irvine gave Jaguar the first podium finish in its F1 history

IRVINE IS ALWAYS A FACTOR IN MONACO, QUICK AND MISTAKE-FREE

From the back, he soon caught Enrique Bernoldi's Arrows, behind which he was trapped all the way until the Brazilian's pit stop on lap 44 of 78.

Forced to circulate some 3.5s slower than his McLaren's true pace, he was lapped by Schumacher well before half-distance.

Coulthard knew that championship challenges are about finishing. He wasn't about to knock the nose off and you can argue that the restraint to frustration ratio was admirable.

"Two years ago I'd probably have put him very deep into the harbour," DC said, "but I'm a bit older and wiser now."

Afterwards, Bernoldi faced a rather sour-faced welcome party, comprising Dennis and Mercedes Motorsport boss Norbert Haug. "I thought that a driver in 15th position who is effectively chopping across the front of a driver contesting the world championship is acceptable for a period of time, but not for as long as it happened," Dennis said.

"What was the objective? If the team is so desperate for television coverage that it has to resort to those strategies. . ."

As Dennis gave his views to a press scrum, an Italian spectator, close to the paddock fence, insisted on shouting over the top of him. Ron asked for a bit of hush but the guy heckled back: "Hey Ron, we are not in a church and you are not Jesus Christ."

Arrows boss Tom Walkinshaw took issue with the punter though. He thought that Ron was doing a very passable impersonation of JC. He said: "I'm going to see if I can borrow some of his magic dust to spray on the water, so that I can walk across to our boat rather than having to get the tender."

And so ended an acrimonious afternoon. Behind Coulthard, barely noticed, Jean Alesi claimed the final point for Prost after one of his typically strong Monaco performances. ■

QUALITY STREETS

Everybody knows about the Monaco Grand Prix, a diamond-crusted anachronism that defies all modern safety criteria but which cannot be erased from the Formula One map.

Monte Carlo at grand prix time can be a pain. The roads are snarled solid and the only sensible modes of transport are scooters (not that sensible, because even small gaps in traffic are hard to find) and shoes. Unless you are staying aboard a harbour-based yacht, be prepared to slog up and down throughout your stay.

For all that Monaco's conspicuous consumption can be distasteful, however, it generates a unique sensory experience. Nowhere else can fans get so close to the action. And while average lap speeds might be relatively slow compared to other tracks, to the naked eye it all looks ridiculously fast. Especially when you stand trackside.

Perch by the exit of the tunnel and the ground shakes perceptibly every time an indistinct blur of noise and colour screams past about six feet away at approximately 170mph. Turn your head to the left in time and you'll see the rear of the car twitching over a crest as its driver starts to think about scrubbing off speed for the piddling chicane that follows. It is the ultimate evidence that computer simulations aren't really simulations at all. Indeed, see this and you doubt they'll ever come close.

Such viewpoints, sadly, are not a privilege you can buy. But it is worth training as a writer, photographer or marshal, just to experience it once in your life.

ACCESS RATING FOR BRITS ★★★★

Travel by train, cab or helicopter from Nice airport (and the latter is better value than you might imagine – cheaper than a taxi if travelling solo). Hotels need to be booked several millennia in advance, however, and they don't half hike up their rates at GP time

STARTING GRID

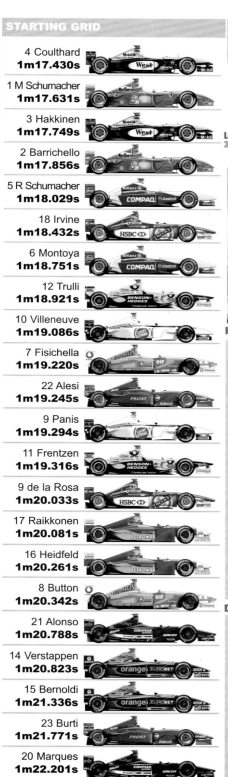

Pos	Driver	Time
4	Coulthard	1m17.430s
1	M Schumacher	1m17.631s
3	Hakkinen	1m17.749s
2	Barrichello	1m17.856s
5	R Schumacher	1m18.029s
18	Irvine	1m18.432s
6	Montoya	1m18.751s
12	Trulli	1m18.921s
10	Villeneuve	1m19.086s
7	Fisichella	1m19.220s
22	Alesi	1m19.245s
9	Panis	1m19.294s
11	Frentzen	1m19.316s
9	de la Rosa	1m20.033s
17	Raikkonen	1m20.081s
16	Heidfeld	1m20.261s
8	Button	1m20.342s
21	Alonso	1m20.788s
14	Verstappen	1m20.823s
15	Bernoldi	1m21.336s
23	Burti	1m21.771s
20	Marques	1m22.201s

May 27 2001
MONTE CARLO STREET CIRCUIT
CIRCUIT LENGTH: 2.094miles / 3.370km

VIRAGE ANTHONY NOGHES
110/177 ②

160/258 ⑥

STE DÉVOTE
50/81 ②

TABAC 95/153 ④

La RASCASSE
30/48 ①

NOUVELLE CHICANE 25/40 ②

MONTÉE de BEAU RIVAGE
160/258 ⑥

165/266 ②

CASINO SQUARE

GRAND HOTEL HAIRPIN
15/24 ①

MIRABEAU 25/40 ②

TUNNEL

VIRAGE du PORTIER
45/72 ②

mph/kmh
② gear

RACE CLASSIFICATION

Pos	Driver	Nat	Car	Laps	Time
1	Michael Schumacher	D	Ferrari F2001-Ferrari V10	78	1h47m22.561s
2	Rubens Barrichello	BR	Ferrari F2001-Ferrari V10	78	+0.431s
3	Eddie Irvine	GB	Jaguar R2-Ford Cosworth V10	78	+30.698s
4	Jacques Villeneuve	CDN	BAR 003-Honda V10	78	+32.454s
5	David Coulthard	GB	McLaren MP4-16-Mercedes V10		+1 lap
6	Jean Alesi	F	Prost AP04-Acer V10		+1 lap
7	Jenson Button	GB	Benetton B201-Renault V10		+1 lap
8	Jos Verstappen	NL	Arrows A22-Asiatech V10		+1 lap
9	Enrique Bernoldi	BR	Arrows A22-Asiatech V10		+2 laps
10	Kimi Raikkonen	FIN	Sauber C20-Petronas V10		+5 laps

Retirements	Nat	Car	Laps	Reason
Ralf Schumacher	D	Williams FW23-BMW V10	57	electronics
Tarso Marques	BR	Minardi PS01-European V10	56	driveshaft
Fernando Alonso	E	Minardi PS01-European V10	54	gearbox
Heinz-Harald Frentzen	D	Jordan EJ11-Honda V10	49	accident
Giancarlo Fisichella	I	Benetton B201-Renault V10	43	gearbox / accident
Jarno Trulli	I	Jordan EJ11-Honda V10	30	electronics
Luciano Burti	BR	Prost AP04-Acer V10	24	brakes / gearbox
Pedro de la Rosa	E	Jaguar R2-Ford Cosworth V10	18	hydraulics
Mika Hakkinen	FIN	McLaren MP4-16-Mercedes V10	15	suspension
Olivier Panis	F	BAR 003-Honda V10	13	steering
Juan Pablo Montoya	CO	Williams FW23-BMW V10	2	accident
Nick Heidfeld	D	Sauber C20-Petronas V10	0	accident

FASTEST LAP D Coulthard 1m19.424s lap 68 (94.914mph / 152.750kmh)

DRIVERS' CHAMPIONSHIP

1	Michael Schumacher	52
2	David Coulthard	40
3	Rubens Barrichello	24
4	Ralf Schumacher	12
5	Nick Heidfeld	8
6	Jacques Villeneuve	7
	Jarno Trulli	7
8	Juan Pablo Montoya	6
	Heinz-Harald Frentzen	6
10	Olivier Panis	5
11	Eddie Irvine	4
	Mika Hakkinen	4
	Kimi Raikkonen	4
14	Giancarlo Fisichella	1
	Jos Verstappen	1
	Jean Alesi	1

CONSTRUCTORS' CHAMPIONSHIP

1	Ferrari	76
2	McLaren-Mercedes	44
3	Williams-BMW	18
4	Jordan-Honda	13
5	Sauber-Petronas	12
	BAR-Honda	12
7	Jaguar-Ford Cosworth	4
8	Benetton-Renault	1
	Arrows-Asiatech	1
	Prost-Acer	1

BROTHERS
FIRST AND
SECOND IN A
GRAND PRIX.
AN EXTRAORDINARY
FEAT AND, ON THE DAY HISTORY
WAS MADE, IT WAS RALF NOT
MICHAEL WHO HAD THE EDGE

GRAND PRIX AIR CANADA

THESE FUELLISH THINGS: having toyed with his brother during the first part of the race, Ralf makes his vital first stop before rejoining at the head of the pack. Inset, time to compare notes for the first siblings ever to have finished 1-2 in a grand prix

IN QUALIFYING THERE WAS LITTLE HINT OF WHAT LAY ahead. Michael Schumacher looked serene, as ever. The Ferrari team leader took his sixth pole in eight races and had more than half a second in hand over his brother's Williams-BMW. Any hopes of an interesting race surely lay with Ralf using BMW grunt to beat Michael to the first corner.

But following the plot was becoming increasingly difficult, muddied by those four round, black things at each corner.

Williams, frankly, was a good bet for pole here. Montreal is all about flat-out blasts between heavy braking for chicanes and hairpins. Power apart, you need a chassis to be strong under braking and you want to be able to ride the kerbs. Michael was obviously in good shape on all counts.

When the Ferrari made it through the first turn ahead, it appeared a certain case of game over. But Ralf had other ideas. He adopted a watching brief and found that he could stay with Michael. More than that, he could stay with him without undue effort.

What was the difference? Well, Sunday afternoon was considerably warmer than the qualifying hour and it is a characteristic of the Michelins that they work much better with a

RALF ADOPTED A WATCHING BRIEF AND FOUND THAT HE COULD STAY WITH MICHAEL. MORE THAN THAT, HE COULD STAY WITH HIM WITHOUT UNDUE EFFORT

EMPTY VESSELS: this season's top three pieces of kit in parc fermé (right) after Hakkinen had trailed the Schueys home to record his first podium finish of the year. Coulthard is spared having to cope with a wonky chassis when his Merc blows (top). Heidfeld mashes a Sauber (above). Raikkonen fizzes with emotion after finishing fourth (above left). Alesi (left) pilfered a pair of points for penniless Prost — and alliteration on that scale is henceforth banned from this book

higher track temperature. Suddenly Ralf found an almost perfect balance with grip to spare.

"The whole time I was waiting for Michael to make a mistake, but he didn't," Ralf said. "I thought we would be able to run longer before making our pit stop and it worked out that way. I wasn't taking a cautious approach because it was Michael, but because I had the upper hand for the whole stint. I was following him easily and my car was brilliant today. I thought the best thing to do was to wait for the pit stops rather than risk sending us straight on at the final chicane." The Williams driver had a look a couple of times there, but Michael braked late and deep, so Ralf thought better of it.

The pair broke the competition easily, but had to do it all over again after Juan Pablo Montoya lost control of his Williams and was collected by Rubens Barrichello, which brought out the Safety Car on lap 20.

As the official Mercedes pulled back into the pits Michael went for it and quickly established a three-second cushion. But as soon as Ralf's Michelin's were cleaned up, he closed effortlessly back onto the Ferrari's gearbox. Michael knew the game was up. When the lead Ferrari stopped on lap 46, Ralf immediately set the fastest lap of the race. Despite Michael setting his own best time first lap out on fresh rubber, the extra five laps that the Williams ran proved decisive and Ralf emerged with a five-second lead.

The only question was whether the new Michelins would enable him to maintain his advantage and we soon had the answer as he

FLARE CANADA

Jacques Villeneuve had a nightmare home race in the Canadian Grand Prix. The British American Racing driver's weekend started badly on Friday when he had a spat with Juan Pablo Montoya over an on-track altercation just before the French-Canadian's session-ending shunt.

It was not the first time that the pair had been involved on the circuit since Montoya's arrival in F1. This time they clashed in the afternoon drivers' briefing when Montoya, who accused Villeneuve of brake-testing him at the hairpin said: "Do that again and I'll put you in the ****ing wall."

According to *Le Journal de Montréal*, Villeneuve retorted with: "I'll put you in the ****ing trees," whereupon the row escalated until Villeneuve grabbed Montoya round the throat and they had to be separated by Williams team manager Dickie Stanford.

FIA race delegate Charlie Whiting sat them down and warned them that any further trouble on Sunday afternoon would result in a ban (Villeneuve had qualified 9th and Montoya 10th).

In the event, Villeneuve's anti-stall system kicked in on the grid and he limped off the line and came around 15th at the end of lap one. He was finally sidelined by a driveshaft problem. BAR team-mate Olivier Panis was a competitive 5th early on before running out of brakes.

Montoya, meanwhile, struggled on the circuit as well as with JV. A gearbox problem robbed him of track time on Friday and he couldn't get within a second of Ralf in qualifying. Then came another shunt, his third incident in as many races. Heading towards the second half of the season, a turnaround was badly needed.

CAPTION SCARLET: Barrichello lines up Trulli; neither proved to be indestructible

BARRICHELLO, ON A LIGHTER FUEL LOAD AND A TWO-STOP STRATEGY, HAD BEEN ABLE TO RUN WITH THE SCHUMACHERS EARLY ON AFTER DIVING PAST COULTHARD

started to extend his lead. Michael knew he was beaten, backed right off and finished 20s down. He was philosophical. "Ralf's the best guy to lose to if it has to be anyone," he said. "I guess mum and dad will be pretty proud of us. I took six points, he got his second win – a happy family day.

"There will be times when this happens. I was working hard but the car was nervous and I could see that Ralf was having an easier time. But we were the best Bridgestone package, quick compared to McLaren, and we can't really ask for more. Sometimes the Michelins will be better. Williams has a good car, Ralf is a good driver and so I've got no problem with it at all."

Barrichello, on a lighter fuel load and a two-stop strategy, had been able to run with the Schumachers early on after diving past Jarno Trulli's Jordan and David Coulthard's McLaren, but he spun coming out of the final hairpin while trying to stay close enough to the powerful BMW to get a run at Ralf into the final hairpin. He resumed 15th and was caught up in Montoya's woes.

Mika Hakkinen scored his first podium of the season, but was a distant third. David Coulthard had a nightmare afternoon with a McLaren afflicted by a suspension problem. He was brave to carry on and lost three points when the engine blew.

Kimi Raikkonen was superb once again, bringing his Sauber home fourth for the second time in three races. Jean Alesi scored another two points for Prost, but poor Jos Verstappen was robbed of a point when his Arrows ran out of brakes three laps from home. Pedro de la Rosa was the benefactor. ∎

DEEP PURPLE HAZE

The Circuit Gilles Villeneuve is a track like no other on the Formula One calendar.

Winding its way up and down an island in the middle of Montreal's St Lawrence Seaway, it is cramped but picturesque – and 2001's combination of bright sunshine and a fresh river breeze made it one of the most convivial settings of the campaign. It is also a magnet for wildlife: Silverstone has its hares, Austria its cows and Canada its gophers, which occasionally poke their noses out from behind the tyre walls to see what the fuss is all about.

The facilities might be a throwback, but would you prefer to tramp around through the woods at Hockenheim or dabble your toes in the drink on a summer afternoon? Thought so.

The best bit of Canada, however, was the exchange rate. With most CDs costing less than 20 dollars, and at 2.2 local dollars to the pound, Montreal's music shops were packed with rabid European visitors throughout the weekend.

True, the composition of the sales racks was a little unusual – Deep Purple appeared to be more relevant in Canada 2001 than they were in London 1971 – but there was no shortage of desirable bargains. And besides, despite the jibe we made about them in our Australian GP report, if you don't yet own a Deep Purple album featuring *Highway Star*, it's about time you did.

ACCESS RATING FOR BRITS ✱✱✱
All the usual caveats about having to deal with the UK's tiresome airports apply, but the flight is less than six hours – and once you arrive it's a cinch to travel by cab and/or public transport. Recommended

STARTING GRID

1 M Schumacher
1m15.782s

5 R Schumacher
1m16.297s

4 Coulthard
1m16.423s

12 Trulli
1m16.459s

2 Barrichello
1m16.760s

9 Panis
1m16.771s

17 Raikkonen
1m16.875s

3 Hakkinen
1m16.979s

10 Villeneuve
1m17.035s

6 Montoya
1m17.123s

16 Heidfeld
1m17.165s

11 Zonta
1m17.328s

14 Verstappen
1m17.903s

19 de la Rosa
1m18.015s

18 Irvine
1m18.016s

22 Alesi
1m18.178s

15 Bernoldi
1m18.575s

7 Fisichella
1m18.622s

23 Burti
1m18.753s

8 Button
1m19.033s

20 Marques
1m20.690s

21 Alonso
0m0.000s

June 10 2001
CIRCUIT GILLES VILLENEUVE, ÎLE NOTRE DAME,
MONTREAL CIRCUIT LENGTH: 2.747miles / 4.421km

mph/kmh
② gear

L'ÉPINAGEE 35/56 ❶

180/290 ⑥   60/97 ②   VIRAGE DU CASINO

150/241 ⑥   PONT DE LA CONCORDE 55/89 ②   195/314 ⑥

70/113 ②   65/105 ②

180/290 ⑥

SENNA CORNER
ISLAND HAIRPIN
30/48 ❶

RACE CLASSIFICATION

Pos	Driver	Nat	Car	Laps	Time
1	Ralf Schumacher	D	Williams FW23-BMW V10	69	1h34m31.522s
2	Michael Schumacher	D	Ferrari F2001-Ferrari V10	69	+20.235s
3	Mika Hakkinen	FIN	McLaren MP4-16-Mercedes V10	69	+40.672s
4	Kimi Raikkonen	FIN	Sauber C20-Petronas V10	69	+1m08.116s
5	Jean Alesi	F	Prost AP04-Acer V10	69	+1m10.435s
6	Pedro de la Rosa	E	Jaguar R2-Ford Cosworth V10		+1 lap
7	Ricardo Zonta*	BR	Jordan EJ11-Honda V10		+1 lap
8	Luciano Burti	BR	Prost AP04-Acer V10		+1 lap
9	Tarso Marques	BR	Minardi PS01-European V10		+3 laps
10	Jos Verstappen	NL	Arrows A22-Asiatech V10		+4 laps
11	Jarno Trulli	I	Jordan EJ11-Honda V10		+6 laps

Ricardo Zonta* took over on Saturday because Heinz-Harald Frentzen was ruled out by illness

Retirements	Nat	Car	Laps	Reason
David Coulthard	GB	McLaren MP4-16-Mercedes V10	54	engine
Olivier Panis	F	BAR 003-Honda V10	38	brakes
Jacques Villeneuve	CDN	BAR 003-Honda V10	34	driveshaft
Enrique Bernoldi	BR	Arrows A22-Asiatech V10	24	engine overheating
Juan Pablo Montoya	CO	Williams FW23-BMW V10	19	accident
Rubens Barrichello	BR	Ferrari F2001-Ferrari V10	19	accident
Jenson Button	GB	Benetton B201-Renault V10	17	oil leak
Fernando Alonso	E	Minardi PS01-European V10	7	driveshaft
Nick Heidfeld	D	Sauber C20-Petronas V10	1	accident
Eddie Irvine	GB	Jaguar R2-Ford Cosworth V10	1	accident
Giancarlo Fisichella	I	Benetton B201-Renault V10	0	accident

FASTEST LAP   R Schumacher 1m17.205s lap 50 (128.094mph / 206.147kmh)

DRIVERS' CHAMPIONSHIP

1	Michael Schumacher	58
2	David Coulthard	40
3	Rubens Barrichello	24
4	Ralf Schumacher	22
5	Mika Hakkinen	8
	Nick Heidfeld	8
7	Jacques Villeneuve	7
	Jarno Trulli	7
	Kimi Raikkonen	7
10	Juan Pablo Montoya	6
	Heinz-Harald Frentzen	6
12	Olivier Panis	5
13	Eddie Irvine	4
14	Jean Alesi	3
15	Giancarlo Fisichella	1
	Jos Verstappen	1
	Pedro de la Rosa	1

CONSTRUCTORS' CHAMPIONSHIP

1	Ferrari	82
2	McLaren-Mercedes	48
3	Williams-BMW	28
4	Sauber-Petronas	15
5	Jordan-Honda	13
6	BAR-Honda	12
7	Jaguar-Ford Cosworth	5
8	Prost-Acer	3
9	Benetton-Renault	1
	Arrows-Asiatech	1

Alonso qualified 21st in 1m 19.454s but the time was disallowed due to the front wing being below the regulated height

WARSTEINER GRAND PRIX OF EUROPE

MONTREAL MIGHT HAVE BEEN
RALF'S, BUT MICHAEL GOT HIS
REVENGE AT THE NÜRBURGRING.
LITTLE BROTHER WAS HIT BY
A STOP-GO PENALTY, BUT THAT WAS
LESS A CAUSE FOR COMPLAINT
THAN HIS SIBLING'S HEAVY-HANDED
DEFENCE AT THE START

GOODY, TWO SCHUEYS: thousands of Germans look on approvingly as Michael and Ralf dominate the early stages (main shot). Schuey Snr earns zillions — and probably doesn't have to pay for his Oakley shades, either (inset).

THERE HAD BEEN A GOOD BATTLE BETWEEN THE brothers in Canada; Ralf's package was superior and so he won. At the Nürburgring, on home territory, Michael nabbed pole once again but the Williams-BMWs were quicker than Rubens and, in race conditions, many suspected that they might be in the pound seats.

The start was crucial. Ralf was wearing used rubber to eliminate the "trough" that was characteristic of Michelin's tyres during the early laps. Michael knew that his brother would be quick in the opening stages. The Ferrari team leader was also on a two-stop strategy, but wasn't sure about Williams. He knew that to get trapped behind an FW23 could blow his race.

The first few yards were controversial. Michael got away smartly, but Ralf used his BMW's extra horses to good effect and was pulling alongside on the inside for the first turn. Michael moved very deliberately to the right, ushering the Williams towards the pit wall to the extent that Ralf was forced to lift momentarily. Sure, Michael had been ahead and thus technically within his rights. But it was still defence of the Vinny Jones variety. Intimidatory, at the very least.

And all this after BMW had already helped him out. . .

Ferrari had a problem with its T-car in the morning warm-up and, as the pit lane opened at 13.30, the team wanted to check its fix. Michael started out on an installation lap only for the car to leave him stranded at the Dunlop Curve, the farthest point from the

IN THE EARLY LAPS THE FERRARI WAS ABLE TO EDGE AWAY FROM THE WILLIAMS PAIR BUT, AS THE RACE DEVELOPED, MICHELIN'S TYRES BEGAN TO HAVE AN EDGE AND RALF CLOSED ONTO MICHAEL'S GEARBOX

pits. With the pits due to close at 13.45, he needed to find transport. And sharpish. He came upon one of BMW's roofed C1 motorcycles, which he quickly commandeered. But there were no keys. Presently, they arrived and as Michael rode back, helmet still on, you could feel the collective sharpening of BMW copywriting pencils.

In the early laps the Ferrari was able to edge away from the Williams pair but, as the race developed, Michelin's tyres began to have an edge and Ralf closed onto Michael's gearbox.

It seemed as if a repeat of Canada was on the cards, but this time the Ferrari and Williams dived in together for their first stops, on lap 28. Michael left his decision late and waited until he saw Ralf heading for the pits in his mirrors before diving across the chevrons that separate pit lane from track. He had to stop Ralf getting the opportunity to run on a clear track. While everyone debated the legality of the move, few noticed Ralf cross the pit lane exit line prematurely on rejoining.

What Michael did was fine, but what Ralf did was not. Schuey Jnr's race was ruined by a 10-second stop-go penalty, which left the way clear for Montoya to emerge an unchallenged second. As Michael backed off in the closing stages, the Colombian got to within 4.2s at the flag.

GUN SAUBER PLOT, clockwise from above: Swiss bloke's cars unusually failed to score; Ralf in reflective pose; Irvine chases Frentzen; Verstappen – small, but perfectly framed; Schuey Snr goes joyriding

BERYLLIUM THE PERIL

Suddenly, McLaren seemed to be struggling. Williams-BMW won in Canada and was the biggest threat to Ferrari again at the Nürburgring. McLaren was in trouble, especially in qualifying.

"The problem is complex," said technical director Adrian Newey (above), "and if it was simple we would have sorted it out. Generally it seems that we are reasonably competitive in races but not in qualifying. And if you don't qualify well you have a difficult Sunday afternoon."

As well as that, of course, there was all the fuss about Newey and his on-off-on-off move to Jaguar. This had undoubtedly destabilised McLaren and the team lost a bit of its formidable focus, but there was more to it than that.

Part of it surrounded the engine. More emphasis was placed on driveability this year than top-end power, but then two things happened. First, traction control was legalised, which meant that driveability was no longer such an issue. And the ban on beryllium hit McLaren harder than anyone.

Beryllium had been an ideal material for engine builders because its density is low but its resistance is very high and its thermal conductivity probably better than any other metals. "So," said an engine man, "for the piston itself it is probably the definition of the perfect material. The big problem is that beryllium dust can be dangerous for a certain amount of the population. The logistical problems are complex and in some countries you might even have a problem handling it. The beryllium itself is not dangerous, it's the machining of it.

"There was a question in the past that if you had an engine seizure on the track, with a lot of smoke coming from the engine, the smoke could be dangerous. There are moral and ethical questions but, in the end, I think it was mostly about performance reduction between teams – typical F1 politics."

SINGLY RED: Barrichello had a lonely last few laps after running wide

STILL SEETHING ABOUT THE START, SCHUEY MkII WAS RATHER LESS EFFUSIVE: "I DON'T WANT TO COMMENT BECAUSE I MIGHT REGRET WHAT I SAY. . ." HE SAID, STROPPILY

"Nothing can be better than winning your home grand prix," said Michael, beaming. "We have had a perfect weekend and I was having a good battle until Ralf got his penalty. We drive close to the edge and I would do this with anyone. We have made it difficult for each other in past races but we always leave room. Today I was a bit slow on the first set of tyres but we changed the balance of the car on the second set and we were much faster. Ralf was unlucky with the penalty. Without that it would have been close but I think I could have done it anyway."

Still seething about the start, Schuey MkII was rather less effusive: "I don't want to comment because I might regret what I say. . ." he said, stroppily.

The McLarens, running a single-stop strategy, were shy of the pace, but Coulthard took advantage of Schumacher Jnr's faux pas to claim the final podium spot, while Ralf recovered to salvage fourth.

Barrichello also stopped just the once. He looked like challenging Ralf's Williams in the final laps, until he went off across the grass at the first corner just after recording his fastest lap.

Mika Hakkinen had an uninspired race, reminiscent of his performance here two years earlier. Although he claimed the final point, he was more than a minute behind the winning Ferrari at the flag. Eddie Irvine's Jaguar, the last unlapped runner, finished just 1.3s behind the Finn. ∎

LAP OF THE GODS

Nowadays, it is hard to find much in the way of entertainment for a fiver. An off-peak cinema ticket? A second-hand CD copy of *Vital*, Van Der Graaf Generator's fine – but underrated – live album? A cup of coffee with a stupid name ("Tall skinny half-toasted latte with elk and walnuts, please")?

It is easy, however, at the Nürburgring.

Next to the circuit lie 14.2 miles of concrete that rise, twist and dip through dense forestation: the Nordschleife. This was the original Nürburgring, built in the late 1920s and home to the German GP until 1976, when current Jaguar boss Niki Lauda crashed his Ferrari and suffered serious injuries that almost killed him. On safety grounds, it was closed to F1 from then on.

It is still used occasionally for racing, however, and for about five quid per lap it is accessible to the general public (apart from Dutchmen towing caravans). Expert motorcyclists mix with semi-professional racers in highly-tuned hatchbacks and tourists ambling along in those engagingly noisy (but slow) three-cylinder Opel Corsas loved by European hire car companies. It is an intoxicating but edgy cocktail: the casualty rate is high, especially among the biking community, but treat it with respect and you will be fine.

The opportunity to say that you have covered the same terrain as Bernd Rosemeyer, Alberto Ascari, Juan Manuel Fangio, Stirling Moss, Jim Clark, Jackie Stewart and hundreds more bygone heroes is irresistible, even just for a lap.

ACCESS RATING FOR BRITS *****

The two Nürburgrings are not far from Spa, Belgium, and can be easily accessed by car in conjunction with boat, 'plane or train. Apart from racing or wild boar hunting, however, be warned that there is absolutely nothing to do for miles

STARTING GRID

1 M Schumacher
1m14.960s

5 R Schumacher
1m15.226s

6 Montoya
1m15.490s

2 Barrichello
1m15.622s

4 Coulthard
1m15.717s

3 Hakkinen
1m15.776s

12 Trulli
1m16.138s

11 Frentzen
1m16.376s

17 Raikkonen
1m16.402s

16 Heidfeld
1m16.438s

10 Villeneuve
1m16.439s

18 Irvine
1m16.588s

9 Panis
1m16.872s

22 Alesi
1m17.251s

7 Fisichella
1m17.378s

19 de la Rosa
1m17.627s

23 Burti
1m18.113s

15 Bernoldi
1m18.151s

14 Verstappen
1m18.262s

8 Button
1m18.626s

21 Alonso
1m18.630s

20 Marques
1m18.689s

June 24 2001
NÜRBURGRING, NÜRBURG/ EIFEL, GERMANY
CIRCUIT LENGTH: 2.831miles / 4.556km

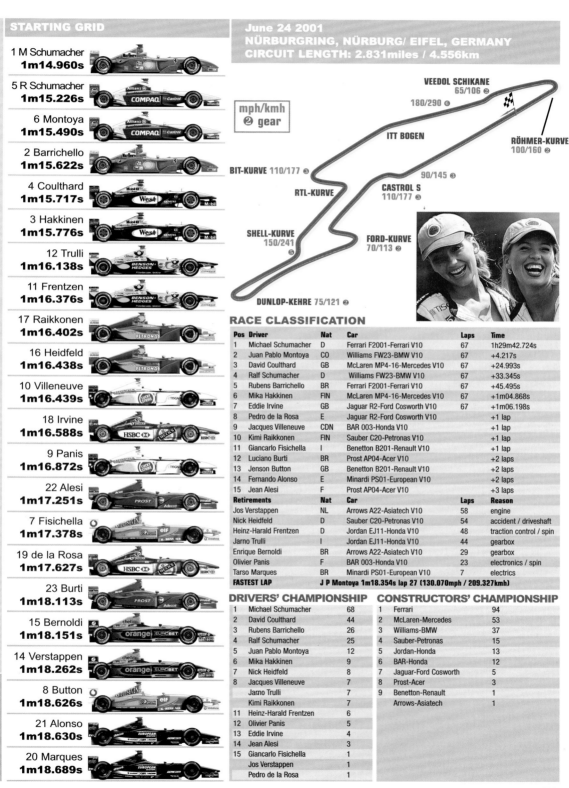

mph/kmh
② gear

VEEDOL SCHIKANE 65/106 ②
180/290 ⑥
ITT BOGEN
RÖHMER-KURVE 100/160 ②
BIT-KURVE 110/177 ③
90/145 ③
RTL-KURVE
CASTROL S 110/177 ③
SHELL-KURVE 150/241 ⑤
FORD-KURVE 70/113 ②
DUNLOP-KEHRE 75/121 ②

RACE CLASSIFICATION

Pos	Driver	Nat	Car	Laps	Time
1	Michael Schumacher	D	Ferrari F2001-Ferrari V10	67	1h29m42.724s
2	Juan Pablo Montoya	CO	Williams FW23-BMW V10	67	+4.217s
3	David Coulthard	GB	McLaren MP4-16-Mercedes V10	67	+24.993s
4	Ralf Schumacher	D	Williams FW23-BMW V10	67	+33.345s
5	Rubens Barrichello	BR	Ferrari F2001-Ferrari V10	67	+45.495s
6	Mika Hakkinen	FIN	McLaren MP4-16-Mercedes V10	67	+1m04.868s
7	Eddie Irvine	GB	Jaguar R2-Ford Cosworth V10	67	+1m06.198s
8	Pedro de la Rosa	E	Jaguar R2-Ford Cosworth V10		+1 lap
9	Jacques Villeneuve	CDN	BAR 003-Honda V10		+1 lap
10	Kimi Raikkonen	FIN	Sauber C20-Petronas V10		+1 lap
11	Giancarlo Fisichella	I	Benetton B201-Renault V10		+1 lap
12	Luciano Burti	BR	Prost AP04-Acer V10		+2 laps
13	Jenson Button	GB	Benetton B201-Renault V10		+2 laps
14	Fernando Alonso	E	Minardi PS01-European V10		+2 laps
15	Jean Alesi	F	Prost AP04-Acer V10		+3 laps

Retirements	Nat	Car	Laps	Reason
Jos Verstappen	NL	Arrows A22-Asiatech V10	58	engine
Nick Heidfeld	D	Sauber C20-Petronas V10	54	accident / driveshaft
Heinz-Harald Frentzen	D	Jordan EJ11-Honda V10	48	traction control / spin
Jarno Trulli	I	Jordan EJ11-Honda V10	44	gearbox
Enrique Bernoldi	BR	Arrows A22-Asiatech V10	29	gearbox
Olivier Panis	F	BAR 003-Honda V10	23	electronics / spin
Tarso Marques	BR	Minardi PS01-European V10	7	electrics

FASTEST LAP   J P Montoya 1m18.354s lap 27 (130.070mph / 209.327kmh)

DRIVERS' CHAMPIONSHIP

1	Michael Schumacher	68
2	David Coulthard	44
3	Rubens Barrichello	26
4	Ralf Schumacher	25
5	Juan Pablo Montoya	12
6	Mika Hakkinen	9
7	Nick Heidfeld	8
8	Jacques Villeneuve	7
	Jarno Trulli	7
	Kimi Raikkonen	7
11	Heinz-Harald Frentzen	6
12	Olivier Panis	5
13	Eddie Irvine	4
14	Jean Alesi	3
15	Giancarlo Fisichella	1
	Jos Verstappen	1
	Pedro de la Rosa	1

CONSTRUCTORS' CHAMPIONSHIP

1	Ferrari	94
2	McLaren-Mercedes	53
3	Williams-BMW	37
4	Sauber-Petronas	15
5	Jordan-Honda	13
6	BAR-Honda	12
7	Jaguar-Ford Cosworth	5
8	Prost-Acer	3
9	Benetton-Renault	1
	Arrows-Asiatech	1

MOBIL1 GRAND PRIX DE FRANCE

WILLIAMS AND BMW ON PEAK FORM. A PADDOCK FULL OF AUVERGNE SAUSAGE. MICHELIN'S HOME PATCH. IT ALL POINTED TO ONE THING, BUT THERE ARE NO PRIZES FOR GUESSING WHO UPSET THE FORM BOOK

SUNNY AND HERR: one Schumacher took pole, the other (right) dominated the race. . . Michael's eldest Gina Maria was probably beating her schoolmates at pass-the-parcel, too. Inset, Mumm's the word as Ralf administers the bubbly

THE COMBINATION OF WILLIAMS-BMW AND MICHELIN
had been the most effective force for the past couple of races. They
duly won in Canada, but things hadn't quite worked out at the
Nürburgring. France, though, appeared to be theirs for the taking.

Williams had dominated the previous test and the weather was
almost certain to be hot – aka Michelin-friendly – on the tyre
giant's home patch. Ralf Schumacher and Juan Pablo Montoya
were backed heavily with the bookies. Dead certs, surely?

But this was Formula One, 2001-style. Not like the early/
mid-Nineties, this, when the only interesting bet was whether the
Williams-Renault would be more than half a minute ahead at
the flag. Sure, Ralf took pole, as the track temperature climbed
helpfully beyond 45degC, but there was Michael's Ferrari just a
hundredth adrift. That was a surprise. He wore a confident smile,
said he felt optimistic for the race and you got the feeling he
wasn't bluffing. Bridgestone, unhappy with its performance here
in the pre-race test, had brought untested new rubber. And it was
just the ticket.

Ralf stormed away from pole and opened up a three-second
lead, but Michael seized the initiative after a shorter first pit stop
and extended his advantage when his brother struggled on his
second set of Michelins. Ralf was never a serious threat again and
looked like he would finish behind team-mate Juan Pablo
Montoya, who had chosen Michelin's harder rubber.

In practice, the Colombian had decided that the softer of
Michelin's two tyre compounds was too much of a gamble
because his car didn't feel particularly stable, a characteristic that
manifested itself through the long, challenging Estoril right-

THE ORDER HAD COME FROM THE PITS FOR RALF EITHER TO PIT OR LET JUAN PABLO BY. FOR FOUR LAPS HE IGNORED IT, CLAIMING HE'D HEARD NOTHING

hander onto the main straight. Montoya knew he would be slower
than Ralf in qualifying but he had a hunch that his was the better
option for Sunday. He was right, but it all became immaterial
when his engine let go.

By that stage, he had already closed onto Ralf's gearbox and the
order had come from the pits for Ralf either to pit or let Juan Pablo
by. For four laps he ignored it, claiming he'd heard nothing due to
radio interference.

In the end it didn't matter. The Bridgestones were consistent
and Michael was gone, helped in part by Ralf's long first pit stop.
In the second stint Schuey Jnr was suddenly a second per lap
slower and his victory hopes evaporated. Michael's biggest worry
had been a clutch problem on the grid. "I nearly lost a position to
David Coulthard," he said. "We came close in the first corner and
if I had been behind him, it could have been a problem for us in
terms of strategy."

There was, of course, a leading car that went nowhere when the
lights changed and – again – it was a McLaren. Mika Hakkinen's
dreadful season continued and thus it was left to DC to uphold the
team's honour. The silver cars were more competitive here than

PIT STROP: Montoya
(above) was the quicker
Williams driver on
Sunday, but his
obstructive team-mate
compromised his
chances – and then his
engine gave up anyway.
**Right, Barrichello
wonders if the word
"David" is big enough on
Coulthard's rear wing**

COMPOUND FROWN

This was supposed to be a banker for Michelin, so what went wrong? In a nutshell, their soft tyre was too soft and their hard too hard.

Ralf Schumacher took the softer option and predictably took pole position. All seemed to be running to plan when he pulled away from his elder brother's Bridgestone-shod Ferrari early on.

"In the first stint I was surprised at how good the balance was," Ralf said. "It was always a concern on the softer rubber, but then after the stops I had understeer and oversteer everywhere. I was sliding all over the circuit, almost parking."

Michelin was at a loss to explain why his second set of rubber was so much worse than the first. Preparation is crucial and the Michelins' early "trough" has to be overcome by scrubbing them in beforehand. Which explained why Ralf was only 17th in the race morning warm-up – he was still busy preparing his tyres. Could it be that he'd simply run out of time?

Not according to Williams technical director Patrick Head, who claimed Ralf had three equally scrubbed sets available for the race.

One of the sets, though, had been used for the fourth qualifying run on Saturday. Even though Ralf didn't use them as hard as he could have done (there was no need, because his pole position was safe), the rubber had still been used harder – and in a higher temperature – than the sets he scrubbed in the morning warm-up.

"That's one possible explanation," Michelin motorsport director Pierre Dupasquier (above) said. "But we're puzzled. The tread depth, temperatures and pressures all absolutely conformed when we took those tyres off. And there was only one lap difference in the preparation, so they were very close indeed. We will check everything carefully to see if the temperatures on the runs in free practice were the same. We just don't know what happened."

STEADY JORDAN: Trulli started fifth – and finished there

PARADISE FOUND

"IT IS A BIG STEP FORWARD FOR MY CHAMPIONSHIP HOPES," MICHAEL SAID IN THE UNDERSTATEMENT OF THE SEASON

in the last two races and, a year on from his great winning drive at Magny-Cours, Coulthard was looking good again. Until, that is, he was a touch over-eager when it came to flicking off his pit lane speed limiter. A 10-second stop-go penalty robbed him of what should have been second place and dropped him to fourth, behind Barrichello's Ferrari.

The Brazilian had switched to a three-stop strategy that, as with so many moves inspired by technical director Ross Brawn, worked out just so. "I was going well in the first stint," Rubens said, "when Ross came on the radio and asked if I wanted to try a three-stop race. It was a good call and I thank the team for that.

"The only problem was that I blistered the rears early on and was struggling to brake. David got very close a couple of times at the Adelaide Hairpin." But not close enough.

Jarno Trulli was the last unlapped runner and took fifth for Jordan-Honda, while Nick Heidfeld kept up the momentum of Sauber's season and collected the final point.

Again, then, tyres had been the determining factor. Bridgestone was delighted to win on Michelin's turf and so was Michael, who brought up his personal half century and moved to within one win of Alain Prost's all-time record 51.

"It is a big step forward for my championship hopes," Michael said in the understatement of the season. He took away a 31-point advantage and, for the rest, it was as good as over.

Then, just to rub it in, he added: "I had a bit of 'flu left over from Nürburgring and I wasn't feeling great. I was pleased that I was able to relax a bit in the last stint." Michelin boss Pierre Dupasquier, meanwhile, was left trying to work out why the German had been afforded that luxury. ■

Popular opinion has it that Magny-Cours is a dump – an anodyne track in the middle of nowhere. But that's harsh.

Although the track is like most of the others on the F1 schedule (ie dull), it has a couple of redeeming features in the shape of Estoril, an ultra-fast right-hander, and Adelaide, a hairpin that permits overtaking (with a little care, admittedly). Actually, come to think of it the downhill chicane just before the pits is quite spectacular, too. So hands off. Magny-Cours is all right, all right?

Besides, while nearby Nevers might not be the most photogenic of towns, the naturescape to the south of the circuit is beyond glorious. Breeze down the RN7 for a dozen miles, find a spot close to the bank of the River Allier, open a bottle of Sancerre and the world doesn't look too bad a place (even before the wine has reached your lips).

Although hotels remain hard to come by, the area is littered with reasonably-priced chateaux within 30 minutes or so of the track. If you want to start your day dunking croissants in fine coffee while watching red squirrels flit across an expansive lawn as swallows dive-bomb unsuspecting midges, then this is the race for you. As the late, great Fred Pontin once said, "Book early."

ACCESS RATING FOR BRITS ★★★★
Easy. The A77 motorway is almost finished and access from the northern French ports is less than five hours by car (unless you are Peter Slater from BBC Radio 5 Live, who left at the busiest possible time and took seven). Trains are a good option, too

STARTING GRID

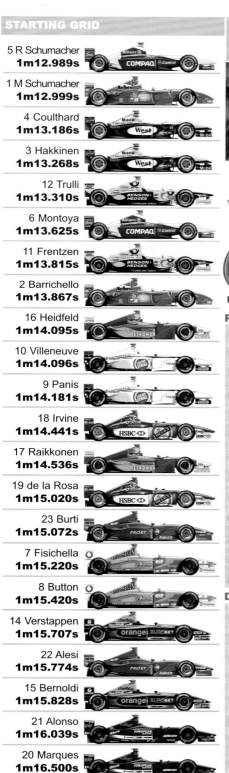

5 R Schumacher
1m12.989s

1 M Schumacher
1m12.999s

4 Coulthard
1m13.186s

3 Hakkinen
1m13.268s

12 Trulli
1m13.310s

6 Montoya
1m13.625s

11 Frentzen
1m13.815s

2 Barrichello
1m13.867s

16 Heidfeld
1m14.095s

10 Villeneuve
1m14.096s

9 Panis
1m14.181s

18 Irvine
1m14.441s

17 Raikkonen
1m14.536s

19 de la Rosa
1m15.020s

23 Burti
1m15.072s

7 Fisichella
1m15.220s

8 Button
1m15.420s

14 Verstappen
1m15.707s

22 Alesi
1m15.774s

15 Bernoldi
1m15.828s

21 Alonso
1m16.039s

20 Marques
1m16.500s

July 1 2001
CIRCUIT NEVERS/MAGNY-COURS
CIRCUIT LENGTH: 2.641miles / 4.251km

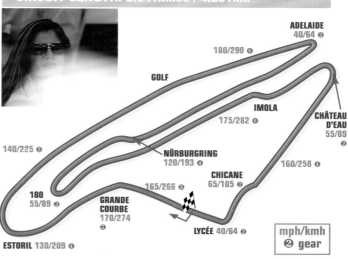

ADELAIDE
40/64 ❷

180/290 ❻

GOLF

IMOLA

CHÂTEAU
D'EAU
55/89
❷

175/282 ❻

140/225 ❺

NÜRBURGRING
120/193 ❹

CHICANE
65/105 ❷

160/258 ❶

180
55/89 ❷

GRANDE
COURBE
170/274
❺

165/266 ❺

LYCÉE 40/64 ❷

mph/kmh
❷ gear

ESTORIL 130/209 ❶

RACE CLASSIFICATION

Pos	Driver	Nat	Car	Laps	Time
1	Michael Schumacher	D	Ferrari F2001-Ferrari V10	72	1h33m35.636s
2	Ralf Schumacher	D	Williams FW23-BMW V10	72	+10.399s
3	Rubens Barrichello	BR	Ferrari F2001-Ferrari V10	72	+16.381s
4	David Coulthard	GB	McLaren MP4-16-Mercedes V10	72	+17.106s
5	Jarno Trulli	I	Jordan EJ11-Honda V10	72	+1m08.285s
6	Nick Heidfeld	D	Sauber C20-Petronas V10		+1 lap
7	Kimi Raikkonen	FIN	Sauber C20-Petronas V10		+1 lap
8	Heinz-Harald Frentzen	D	Jordan EJ11-Honda V10		+1 lap
9	Olivier Panis	F	BAR 003-Honda V10		+1 lap
10	Luciano Burti	BR	Prost AP04-Acer V10		+1 lap
11	Giancarlo Fisichella	I	Benetton B201-Renault V10		+1 lap
12	Jean Alesi	F	Prost AP04-Acer V10		+2 laps
13	Jos Verstappen	NL	Arrows A22-Asiatech V10		+2 laps
14	Pedro de la Rosa	E	Jaguar R2-Ford Cosworth V10		+2 laps
15	Tarso Marques	BR	Minardi PS01-European V10		+3 laps
16	Jenson Button	GB	Benetton B201-Renault V10		+4 laps
17	Fernando Alonso	E	Minardi PS01-European V10		+7 laps

Retirements		Nat	Car	Laps	Reason
Eddie Irvine		GB	Jaguar R2-Ford Cosworth V10	54	engine
Juan Pablo Montoya		CO	Williams FW23-BMW V10	52	engine
Enrique Bernoldi		BR	Arrows A22-Asiatech V10	17	engine
Jacques Villeneuve		CDN	BAR 003-Honda V10	5	electrics
Mika Hakkinen		FIN	McLaren MP4-16-Mercedes V10		did not start due to electronics/engine

FASTEST LAP   D Coulthard 1m16.088s lap 53 (124.977mph / 201.130kmh)

DRIVERS' CHAMPIONSHIP

1	Michael Schumacher	78
2	David Coulthard	47
3	Ralf Schumacher	31
4	Rubens Barrichello	30
5	Juan Pablo Montoya	12
6	Mika Hakkinen	9
	Nick Heidfeld	9
	Jarno Trulli	9
9	Jacques Villeneuve	7
	Kimi Raikkonen	7
11	Heinz-Harald Frentzen	6
12	Olivier Panis	5
13	Eddie Irvine	4
14	Jean Alesi	3
15	Giancarlo Fisichella	1
	Jos Verstappen	1
	Pedro de la Rosa	1

CONSTRUCTORS' CHAMPIONSHIP

1	Ferrari	108
2	McLaren-Mercedes	56
3	Williams-BMW	43
4	Sauber-Petronas	16
5	Jordan-Honda	15
6	BAR-Honda	12
7	Jaguar-Ford Cosworth	5
8	Prost-Acer	3
9	Benetton-Renault	1
	Arrows-Asiatech	1

THAT WAS TH

E YEAR THAT WAS

**MEMORIES LIKE THE CORNERS OF MY MIND
MEMORIES
MISTY WATERCOLOUR MEMORIES
OF THE WAY WE WERE
SCATTERED PICTURES OF THE SMILES WE LEFT BEHIND
SMILES WE GAVE TO ONE ANOTHER
FOR THE WAY WE WERE**

THANK YOU GLADYS KNIGHT. CHANCES ARE THAT SHE WASN'T SINGING ABOUT
Froilan Gonzalez scoring Ferrari's first F1 win 50 years ago, but you never know. Here are a few more notable anniversaries from the past year. Curiously, Gladys has never commemorated any of them in song, either

120 YEARS AGO
SEP 15
Ettore Bugatti **(1)** born. Goes on to make some quite nice cars. The only time a Bugatti started a world championship grand prix was at Reims, France, in 1956, when Maurice Trintignant's T251 retired after 18 laps.

90 YEARS AGO
JUN 24
Juan Manual Fangio **(2)** roars into the world, probably in a masterfully balanced four-wheel drift. Turns out to be quite handy.

80 YEARS AGO
FEB 16
Jean Behra – a natural-born giant-killer – emerges on planet Earth. Loved by the French for heroic deeds at the wheel of a Gordini in the early Fifties. Never won a world championship race, but still an absolute ace.

75 YEARS AGO
NOV 11
Maria Teresa de Filippis born **(3)**. First lady to start a world championship F1 race, at Spa in 1958.

65 YEARS AGO
MAR 4
Mr & Mrs Clark celebrate the birth of their son Jim in Kilmany, Scotland. Odd to think that the double world champion **(main pic)** would be eligible for a bus pass by now, had he lived.

50 YEARS AGO

JAN 1
Hans Stuck **(1)** exhales for the first time. Subsequently a tin-top and sports car hero, with a few spectacular F1 drives thrown in for good measure. Engagingly loopy – and still racing.

MAY 27
Stirling Moss makes his first world championship start at the wheel of an HWM in the Swiss GP at Bremgarten. He finishes eighth, two laps down **(7)**.

JUL 14
Froilan Gonzalez scores Ferrari's maiden grand prix win, at Silverstone **(2)**. In the same race BRM makes its first world championship start and Peter Walker takes the V16-engined P15 to seventh place, just six laps behind Gonzalez.

JUL 29
Alberto Ascari (Ferrari 375) scores his first GP win, at Germany's Nürburgring.

OCT 28
Juan Manuel Fangio clinches his first world title by winning the Spanish GP at Pedralbes. It is also Alfa Romeo's last F1 win. The company has had a few stabs at F1 since, but nowadays concentrates on making glorious but slightly impractical cars (diesels that aren't hugely economical, estates with precious little luggage capacity – that kind of thing).

OCT 29
Tiff Needell (one GP start, lots of TV broadcasts, once drove Nigel Mansell into a bridge during a touring car race) is born one day too late to appreciate Fangio's title. We feel it is important that everyone is made aware that Tiff **(3)** was 50 this year.

40 YEARS AGO

MAR 30
Mike Thackwell born – and begins racing about five minutes later. Just 19 years 5 months and 29 days old when he started the 1980 Canadian GP in Montreal. Lasted

about 100 yards, but entered history as youngest driver ever to take part in a GP.

AUG 6
Stirling Moss records his final GP victory in Rob Walker's Lotus 18/21 at the Nürburgring.

SEP 10
World championship leader Wolfgang von Trips **(4)** is killed in the Italian GP at Monza. His Ferrari team-mate Phil Hill wins – for the last time in F1 – and in so doing clinches the title.

OCT 8
Brits Stirling Moss and Tony Brooks make their final world championship starts in the United States GP at Watkins Glen.

35 YEARS AGO

MAY 22
Bruce McLaren **(8)** gives his eponymous F1 car its first race in Monaco. He qualifies 10th fastest but retires with an oil leak after nine laps.

JUL 3
The glorious Reims circuit **(5)** stages its final world championship race. Basically an amalgam of three public roads, the French track staged its last car race in 1969. The old pit buildings and grandstands remain to this day, charmingly ramshackle and overgrown. Worth a visit – in fact it ought to be mandatory.

30 YEARS AGO

MAR 6
Mario Andretti (Ferrari 312B) scores his first GP win, in South Africa, on only his 10th world championship start **(6)**.

APR 18
At Montjuich Park, Spain, Jackie Stewart gives Tyrrell the first of its 23 GP wins.

AUG 15
At the Österreichring, Niki Lauda makes his first GP start in a hired March 711. He qualifies last and fails to finish – hardly form to suggest there is a future triple world champion in F1's midst.

25 YEARS AGO

JAN 25

Ligier makes its first GP start in Brazil **(1)**, with the fantastic JS5 that looks like a teapot on wheels. Jacques Laffite qualifies it 11th, but broken gear linkage forces him to retire.

AUG 1

Niki Lauda crashes heavily at the old, 14-mile Nürburgring. He is dragged from the flaming wreckage and read the last rites, but is on the grid at Monza about six weeks later. The 'Ring is henceforth banished from the F1 calendar on safety grounds.

SEP 12

Ronnie Peterson scores what proves to be March's last GP win, at Monza.

OCT 24

It rains a lot in Japan and the country's first F1 GP is delayed. James Hunt eventually finishes third to clinch the world title **(7)**. Rival Lauda quits after a couple of laps because he says conditions are too dangerous.

20 YEARS AGO

FEB 28

Joe Dolce's *Shaddap You Face* keeps Ultravox's *Vienna* off the top of UK charts. Not strictly a motor racing fact, but worthy of inclusion on the grounds of general ludicrousness.

MAR 23

Motorcycling hero and former F1 racer Mike Hailwood **(2)** is killed in a road accident. Spends much of his life taming the Isle of Man TT circuit on a 'bike and then perishes on an errand to buy fish and chips. Irony doesn't come much deeper. The sport mourns an all-round good bloke.

JUN 21

Gilles Villeneuve scores his final F1 win at Jarama, Spain, in Ferrari's unwieldy 126CK, a prototype of the TCR jammer car. A large traffic jam follows him across the line and the top five cars are covered by 1.231s.

JUL 5

On home soil at Dijon, Alain Prost (Renault RE30) scores the first of his 51 GP wins **(3)**.

OCT 17

Alan Jones (Williams FW07C) notches up the final F1 win of his career **(4)**, in a Las Vegas car park that passes itself off as a GP track.

15 YEARS AGO

JUL 13

Brands Hatch stages the British GP for the final time before Silverstone nabs it in apparent perpetuity. A startline pile-up **(8)** mars the race. In his 176th start, Jacques Laffite sustains leg injuries that end his F1 career.

AUG 10

F1 breaks new ground by going to Hungary for the first time.

10 YEARS AGO

MAR 10

Jordan makes its first GP start in Phoenix, in what will be the last United States GP until Indianapolis 2000.

JUN 2

Nigel Mansell waves to the Montreal crowd to celebrate his Canadian GP success – and inadvertently allows his engine revs to die, which causes his car to grind to a halt as he exits the last corner. Nelson Piquet cruises by to score the final win of his F1 career and openly laughs at Mansell afterwards. Still is, probably.

AUG 25

With driver Bertrand Gachot unable to race because he has been jailed for using pepper spray on a stroppy London cabbie, Jordan calls up Michael Schumacher to deputise at Spa. He qualifies seventh but fries his clutch shortly after the start. Ten minutes later, Benetton nicks him and lays in place the foundations for glory.

SEP 29

The current Barcelona track stages its first GP, notable for Nigel Mansell and Ayrton

Senna tearing down the main straight half a millimetre apart, at about 190mph **(9)**. Mansell wins.

OCT 20
Senna clinches his third and final F1 title by finishing second to team-mate Gerhard Berger at Suzuka, Japan **(5)**.

5 YEARS AGO

MAR 10
Jacques Villeneuve makes his first F1 start from pole position in Melbourne, Australia.

MAY 19
Olivier Panis wins the Monaco GP from 14th place on the grid. It is Ligier's first win since Canada 1981 – and also its last.

OCT 13
Damon Hill clinches the world title by winning the Japanese GP at Suzuka **(6)**. Bizarrely, only three drivers named Hill have ever taken part in an F1 grand prix – and all of them have been world champion. Damon's predecessors were Phil (no relation, 1961) and Graham (his dad, 1962 and 1968).

FOSTER'S BRITISH GRAND PRIX

HITHERTO
A SHADOW
OF HIS USUAL
SELF, THE REAL
MIKA HAKKINEN
DELIVERED
A FLAWLESS
PERFORMANCE
AT SILVERSTONE.
MIND YOU,
FERRARI'S
TACTICS WERE
SLIGHTLY AWRY
FOR ONCE

HI-HO SILVER SHINING: With Scooby Doo and his mates having exposed the flaky impostor that had been standing in at McLaren, the real Mika Hakkinen returned at Silverstone (right). Inset, Agadoo-doo-doo, push pineapple, shake a tree. . .

THERE WAS A PAT ON THE SHOULDER FOR MIKA HAKKINEN. THE FINN HAD HIS FIRST WIN SINCE SPA AND *THAT* GREAT MOVE ALMOST A YEAR EARLIER

MICHAEL SCHUMACHER AND FERRARI WERE WELL beaten at Silverstone, but the champion didn't seem to mind. There was a pat on the shoulder for Mika Hakkinen and a warm shake of the hand. The Finn had his first win since Spa and *that* great move almost a year earlier.

This one was against the run of play. Suggest in June that Hakkinen and McLaren would dominate the British Grand Prix and the men in white coats would justifiably have been sent for. But, at flag fall, the Finn's MP4/16 was half a minute clear – good news for punters who backed him at a generous 10/1.

If Silverstone was a beacon of brightness amid a maelstrom of misery for Mika, for his team-mate it meant any slim hopes of a tilt at the title being banished to the back of the mind for another year. A coming-together between David Coulthard and Jarno Trulli at Copse, on lap one, led to rear suspension damage that would get the Scot no further than the Bridge Corner gravel trap, on lap three.

At Imola, Montreal, the Nürburgring and Magny-Cours, Michelin's dry rubber had posed a serious threat to the Bridgestone runners and, coming to Silverstone, Ralf Schumacher's Williams-BMW had never qualified outside the top five. Suddenly though, Juan Pablo Montoya and Schuey Jnr were 8th and 10th.

RADIODEAD (above): Team, "Oi, cloth ears. Let Juan Pablo through." Ralf, "Zzzzzz." Coulthard (left) was aiming for a British GP hat trick, but managed only three laps. Burti – apparently looking the wrong way – and Irvine rub wheels (right). Barrichello goes kerb-mauling (far right).

Williams tech director Patrick Head candidly admitted that there was more than rubber behind the team's deficiencies, however.

Chez McLaren, meanwhile, tyres were flavour of the weekend. Hakkinen loved the new Bridgestone, which gave him a front end that stuck, but while tyre performance had decided the previous races, the Silverstone plot was simpler – McLaren stopped twice, Ferrari just the once.

When Schumacher made full use of his pole position and got through Copse in front, Mika knew he had to get by urgently if he was to optimise his strategy. Uncharacteristically, Michael goofed at Copse and gifted him the chance.

Mika accepted gratefully and, once through, was in a race of his own. With Coulthard out, Michael simply stroked to second place and banked a 37-point advantage with just 60 still to play for.

The surprise was that Ferrari and McLaren came up with such different answers to the Silverstone performance equation. It was a close call between one and two stops and Ferrari, for once, seemed to have it wrong.

But Schumacher warned against jumping to conclusions. Without the mistake at Copse, he said, it could have been a different race.

"It's very difficult to overtake at Silverstone unless someone

FINNS AIN'T WHAT THEY USED TO BE

Mika Hakkinen (above) was back and the relief was obvious.

His margin of victory was the big surprise, even if Ferrari was below par. "I wanted to make a big gap and push hard so that I had time for a cup of tea at the end before Michael arrived," he said, teasing gently.

Only a handful of people knew it at the time, but it was a great drive considering Hakkinen's frame of mind. He had first spoken to Ron Dennis at Monaco a few weeks earlier about the prospect of stopping – or at least taking a year out. And the doubts stretched right back to race one in Melbourne, where he was in contention before a big shunt.

"We were looking competitive there, our tactics were good and then all of a sudden I had the big hit. I hurt myself, I had to go to hospital and it cheesed me off, to be honest. I thought, right then, that I had to do something about the feeling I had."

Mika, of course, suffered a near-fatal accident at Adelaide in 1995 and the accident could only have brought back memories, just three months after the arrival of his first-born son, Hugo.

"Being a father has certainly affected the way I see racing," he admitted. "You have your family and your work and you try to do both. But it's a dangerous sport and when you have something in your life that you really don't want to lose, you start to think about that. It's true that when you are young and you cross the road, you look left and right once. But as you get older you look twice."

He worried, of course, about thoughts like that. He was put on earth to drive racing cars and he knew his mind could temper his talent. But Silverstone told him he could overcome it.

PASS RATE: Montoya on the verge of duping the world champ – again

BYPASS SURGERY

FRENTZEN WAS SEVENTH AND EJ'S MIND WAS MADE UP. A FEW DAYS LATER HE SHOWED HEINZ-HARALD THE DOOR

makes a mistake. I made one today but just because I did it once doesn't mean I would have done it twice. Where Mika passed me is not normally an overtaking opportunity. It's generally more important to get out of Becketts well to protect yourself at the end of Hangar Straight, which I was doing."

Silverstone is an away match for Ferrari and technical director Ross Brawn confirmed that somewhat less-than-exhaustive preparation – just two days with two drivers followed by the loss of free practice due to rain – had decided Ferrari's game plan.

"I expected Mika to be on a very aggressive strategy," he said. "David was our opposition and so we adopted 'banker' tactics."

The car, Schumacher said, had never been right. And set-up at Silverstone is vital. "With all the high-speed stuff you don't just lose a couple of hundredths, it goes into tenths. Mika's quickest lap was half a second quicker than mine, which was the true strength of it."

The fast-starting Montoya briefly relegated Schumacher to third going into Copse, on lap 17. "I wasn't concerned though, I was pretty sure he was doing a two-stop race," Michael said.

Montoya was, and after his stop he soon caught the battle between Rubens Barrichello and the one-stopping Schuey Jnr for third. Despite a "switch" pit board from the Williams team, Ralf stayed resolutely where he was until his own stop a handful of laps later. It was immaterial as far as Ralf was concerned – his BMW suffered a sudden power loss and he pulled off on lap 37. But Barrichello maintained his third place, Montoya had to be content with fourth and Williams was less than impressed that Ralf had not allowed Juan Pablo to optimise his strategy. . .

Kimi Raikkonen and Nick Heidfeld made Peter Sauber's day with fifth and sixth places. The Swiss team thus stretched its advantage to four points over the first works Honda team in the bid to finish fourth in the championship for constructors. That was pretty unpalatable for Eddie Jordan's troops on home ground. Frentzen was seventh and EJ's mind was now made up. A few days later he showed Heinz-Harald the door. ∎

Most people with half a clue about racing know that Silverstone began life as a World War Two airfield. And if you didn't, you wouldn't need to spend long on the premises to find evidence of the track's origins.

But things have moved on since it opened in 1948, when cars raced up and down diagonal runways that converged in the middle of the site. TV commentary legend Murray Walker, who made his final British GP broadcast in 2001, was there in the late Forties. "At one point, cars were thundering pretty much towards each other at a closing speed of about 300mph," he says. "All that separated them were a bit of Tarmac and a few oil drums. You really had to be there to appreciate how potentially dangerous it was."

Nowadays Silverstone has several track layouts, all somewhat more sophisticated than the original, and race promoter Octagon has committed to upgrading the facilities totally during the next few years.

What it presently lacks in terms of modern accoutrements, however, Silverstone makes up for with atmosphere – even if you pitch up on a Formula One test day the place tends to be heaving.

If you have never visited the British GP, however, take a tip: make a weekend of it and use one of the nearby camping facilities. True, you might get drenched – but the only sensible ways to get in and out during the race weekend involve motorbikes, pedal cycles or feet.

ACCESS RATING FOR BRITS ★★★★
It is not getting five stars until the new Silverstone bypass is finished. Traffic access improved in 2001, mind: average speeds were up to almost 6mph at one point

STARTING GRID

July 15 2001. SILVERSTONE GRAND PRIX CIRCUIT, TOWCESTER, NORTHAMPTONSHIRE.
CIRCUIT LENGTH: 3.194 miles / 5.141km

1 M Schumacher
1m20.447s

3 Hakkinen
1m20.529s

4 Coulthard
1m20.927s

12 Trulli
1m20.930s

11 Frentzen
1m21.217s

2 Barrichello
1m21.715s

17 Raikkonen
1m22.023s

6 Montoya
1m22.219s

16 Heidfeld
1m22.223s

5 R Schumacher
1m22.283s

9 Panis
1m22.316s

10 Villeneuve
1m22.916s

19 de la Rosa
1m23.273s

22 Alesi
1m23.392s

18 Irvine
1m23.439s

23 Burti
1m23.735s

14 Verstappen
1m24.067s

8 Button
1m24.123s

7 Fisichella
1m24.275s

15 Bernoldi
1m24.606s

21 Alonso
1m24.792s

Did not qualify: Tarso Marques BR Minardi PS01-European V10 **(1m 26.506s)**

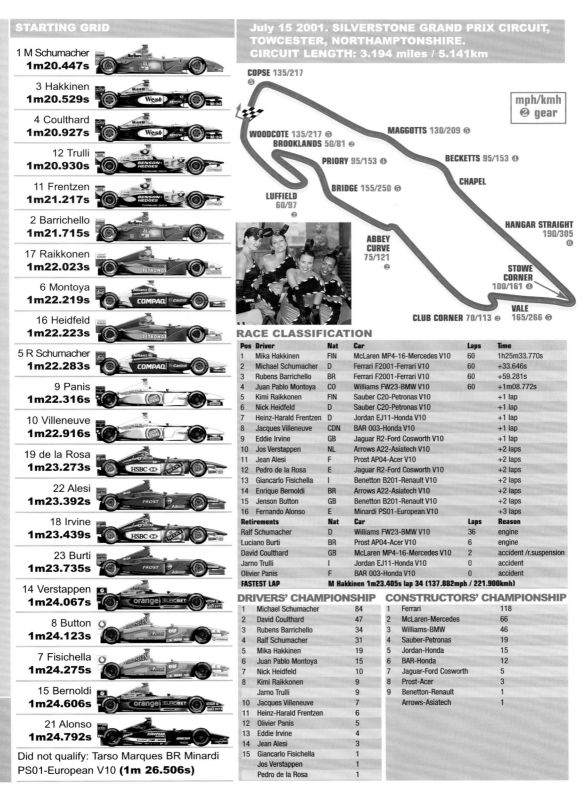

COPSE 135/217 ⑤

WOODCOTE 135/217 ⑤
BROOKLANDS 50/81 ②

MAGGOTTS 130/209 ⑤

PRIORY 95/153 ④

BECKETTS 95/153 ③

CHAPEL

BRIDGE 155/250 ⑤

LUFFIELD 60/97 ②

ABBEY CURVE 75/121 ②

HANGAR STRAIGHT 190/305 ⑥

STOWE CORNER 100/161 ④

CLUB CORNER 70/113 ②

VALE 165/266 ⑤

mph/kmh ② gear

RACE CLASSIFICATION

Pos	Driver	Nat	Car	Laps	Time
1	Mika Hakkinen	FIN	McLaren MP4-16-Mercedes V10	60	1h25m33.770s
2	Michael Schumacher	D	Ferrari F2001-Ferrari V10	60	+33.646s
3	Rubens Barrichello	BR	Ferrari F2001-Ferrari V10	60	+59.281s
4	Juan Pablo Montoya	CO	Williams FW23-BMW V10	60	+1m08.772s
5	Kimi Raikkonen	FIN	Sauber C20-Petronas V10		+1 lap
6	Nick Heidfeld	D	Sauber C20-Petronas V10		+1 lap
7	Heinz-Harald Frentzen	D	Jordan EJ11-Honda V10		+1 lap
8	Jacques Villeneuve	CDN	BAR 003-Honda V10		+1 lap
9	Eddie Irvine	GB	Jaguar R2-Ford Cosworth V10		+1 lap
10	Jos Verstappen	NL	Arrows A22-Asiatech V10		+2 laps
11	Jean Alesi	F	Prost AP04-Acer V10		+2 laps
12	Pedro de la Rosa	E	Jaguar R2-Ford Cosworth V10		+2 laps
13	Giancarlo Fisichella	I	Benetton B201-Renault V10		+2 laps
14	Enrique Bernoldi	BR	Arrows A22-Asiatech V10		+2 laps
15	Jenson Button	GB	Benetton B201-Renault V10		+2 laps
16	Fernando Alonso	E	Minardi PS01-European V10		+3 laps

Retirements	Nat	Car	Laps	Reason
Ralf Schumacher	D	Williams FW23-BMW V10	36	engine
Luciano Burti	BR	Prost AP04-Acer V10	6	engine
David Coulthard	GB	McLaren MP4-16-Mercedes V10	2	accident /r.suspension
Jarno Trulli	I	Jordan EJ11-Honda V10	0	accident
Olivier Panis	F	BAR 003-Honda V10	0	accident

FASTEST LAP M Hakkinen 1m23.405s lap 34 (137.882mph / 221.900kmh)

DRIVERS' CHAMPIONSHIP

1	Michael Schumacher	84
2	David Coulthard	47
3	Rubens Barrichello	34
4	Ralf Schumacher	31
5	Mika Hakkinen	19
6	Juan Pablo Montoya	15
7	Nick Heidfeld	10
8	Kimi Raikkonen	9
	Jarno Trulli	9
10	Jacques Villeneuve	7
11	Heinz-Harald Frentzen	6
12	Olivier Panis	5
13	Eddie Irvine	4
14	Jean Alesi	3
15	Giancarlo Fisichella	1
	Jos Verstappen	1
	Pedro de la Rosa	1

CONSTRUCTORS' CHAMPIONSHIP

1	Ferrari	118
2	McLaren-Mercedes	66
3	Williams-BMW	46
4	Sauber-Petronas	19
5	Jordan-Honda	15
6	BAR-Honda	12
7	Jaguar-Ford Cosworth	5
8	Prost-Acer	3
9	Benetton-Renault	1
	Arrows-Asiatech	1

ER MOBIL 1 PREIS VON DEUTSCHLAND

WITH TWO WILLIAMS-BMWS ON THE FRONT ROW, A FIRED-UP FINN AND SCHUEY SNR JUST BEHIND, IT PROMISED TO BE AN EPIC. BUT THEN LOTS OF ENGINES BLEW UP AND NOTHING MUCH HAPPENED. WELL, APART FROM LUCIANO BURTI CARTWHEELING

MIRROR, SIGNAL, MANOEUVRE. . . OH BUGGER: Schuey hit transmission trouble, Burti hit Schuey. Inset, baby brother had no such concerns

TRADITIONALLY THE GERMAN GRAND PRIX is marked by an explosion of firecrackers from terraces packed with cheery, beery locals. But this time there were just as many engines blowing up.

Winner Ralf Schumacher was asked a simple question. His team-mate Juan Pablo Montoya had led comfortably early on, but the Colombian's BMW V10 eventually expired in a cloud of smoke. How worried was Ralf that he might have suffered the same fate? His answer was mischievous and disingenuous in equal measure.

"I saw how quickly Juan Pablo was going early on," he said, "and I thought, 'If you want to go at that speed, it's up to you'. But I know how hard this place is on engines. At the end, when I had a good lead, I certainly backed off a little to be on the safe side."

The implication was clear. When we saw Montoya blowing Schuey Jnr away in the opening laps, that wasn't what we were seeing at all. It was just the German being cautious – or so he'd have us believe.

The WilliamsF1 (yes, it looks silly squashed up as one word like that, but that's how their marketeers insist it should be) team didn't quite see it that way. Technical director Patrick Head said: "Juan was always driving well within the limits of his engine."

In truth, however, Montoya was beaten before his engine expired. Having stormed away from his first F1 pole position and opened up a handsome lead over Ralf, he was undone when he came in to make his one and only scheduled pit stop. On went the refuelling nozzle – and on it stayed.

Then the team disconnected it and had a go with

BY THE TIME HE REJOINED, MONTOYA HAD ALMOST ENOUGH SPARE FUEL ON BOARD TO GET A BOEING 747 FROM LONDON TO SYDNEY

YELLOW LAG: Trulli – modest in the race, but included here because this is a nice picture (main shot). Right (from left, if you follow): both Benetton drivers bagged points; Montoya leads; de la Rosa being inept

Schuey Jnr's hose. The gauges suggested no fuel had been going in originally – although this wasn't actually the case. By the time he rejoined in fourth place (behind Rubens Barrichello's two-stopping Ferrari), Montoya had almost enough spare fuel on board to get a Boeing 747 from London to Sydney, so he wouldn't have been terribly fast in the latter stages, had he lasted. As in Brazil, victory should have been his for the taking – and for the third successive grand prix he had been quicker than Ralf in race trim.

But it was Schuey Jnr who scored F1 victory number three and climbed to the top of the podium. It had been another controlled performance – and utterly faultless. You just sensed he wished the other Williams hadn't been there as a benchmark early on.

The afternoon started dramatically when Michael Schumacher's Ferrari developed gear selection problems as he left the line. Cars dodged this way and that in avoidance, but the unsighted Luciano Burti

FIRED AND EMOTIONAL

Banners wishing one or both of the Schumacher brothers good luck are common enough in Germany. Trying to find a crumb of support for Heinz-Harald Frentzen or Nick Heidfeld, however, is usually a bit like trying to unearth a Sol Campbell sympathiser at White Hart Lane.

When Jordan axed Frentzen during the build-up to his home race, a local radio station trawled the Hockenheim camp sites for genuine Frentzen fans (rather than mere sympathisers). It found only a couple. There were messages of support, however, for the driver who only two years earlier had improbably kept Jordan in the F1 title hunt almost until the end of the season.

One placard hanging in front of a prominent grandstand was plain enough: "Jordan go home".

Team boss Eddie J wasn't about to disclose why he had pitched Frentzen, but it didn't exactly turn out to be a change for the good.

Jarno Trulli's quest to boost the beleaguered team with a points finish was compromised when he had a silly spin while fighting with the BARs of Olivier Panis and Jacques Villeneuve. His challenge later ended altogether with a hydraulic failure.

Villeneuve? He eventually went on to finish third to put BAR ahead of Jordan in the championship for constructors. As both are official Honda partners, there is much political capital to be made here.

To compound Jordan's misery, Frentzen's stand-in Ricardo Zonta (above) made a poor fist of showing he was the man for the job on a permanent basis. A series of basic errors culminated in him clipping the back of Jos Verstappen in the race.

The fact he was behind an Arrows in the first place speaks volumes.

TWO GRIT: Alonso (background) runs wide to avoid team-mate Marques

CONSPIRACY THEORIES ARE PART AND PARCEL OF F1, BUT THIS TIME THE RED FLAG WAS THE ONLY VALID OPTION

rammed the world championship leader and his Prost somersaulted spectacularly. He flew over the top of Enrique Bernoldi's Arrows, which collected one of Burti's stray wheels on its engine cover.

No one was hurt but the race had to be red-flagged because of the amount of debris on the track – and you don't want tyres picking up carbon shards when cars are streaming along Hockenheim's tree-lined straights at 220mph.

One or two drivers felt it odd that the race should have been stopped, the implication being that it was a convenient excuse to get Schuey Snr back in the race in his spare chassis. Conspiracy theories are part and parcel of F1, but this time the red flag was the only valid option. Michelin motorsport director Pierre Dupasquier admitted he was "terrified" that they might not stop it.

The accident victims duly restarted in their back-up chassis, but not even that stroke of good fortune could help the world championship leader. Along with Montoya and the McLarens of Mika Hakkinen and David Coulthard, Schumacher Snr went out with engine failure and spent the rest of the afternoon listening to the commentary on a marshal's transistor radio. And he couldn't help sniggering when he heard that closest (relatively speaking) title rival Coulthard had gone pop. Barrichello's two-stop strategy didn't look like the best plan on paper, but he drove tidily to pick up second place thanks, in part, to the high rate of attrition. The balance of the top six told you what kind of afternoon it had been, with Jacques Villeneuve, both Benetton drivers and Jean Alesi picking up points.

To be fair to Benetton, Giancarlo Fisichella and Jenson Button both felt the customarily canine B201 was more competitive than it had been all season – although a clutch of problems prevented them qualifying any better than usual. Both raced strongly – and Button overcame the distraction of a loose drinks bottle tube that sprayed his face with liquid every time he braked. ∎

SHORT TRACK ASIDES

This was probably the final German Grand Prix on the old Hockenheim, which is basically a 4.24-mile blast through the woods (apart from the twiddlybit that runs past the main grandstands, obviously).

It might have all the architectural flair of the M11, but Hockenheim at least provides relief from the thou-shalt-not-pass circuits that make up so much of the world championship. Overtaking is seldom a problem and the combination of low downforce set-ups, ultra-high speeds (Mika Hakkinen recorded 223mph through the radar trap after picking up a hefty tow) and heavy braking lend themselves to old-fashioned, cut-and-thrust racing. Even if there wasn't much going on at the front of the field in 2001, there were pockets of excitement elsewhere (Barrichello v Coulthard and Trulli v the BARs spring to mind).

But no more.

If the developers hit their target, an all-new Hockenheim will be ready for June 2002. It features the least interesting bits of the current track and a couple of new sections that will be laid over what is currently dense forestry, so the track is likely to become just another featureless autodrome. Doubtless the Germans will still camp out in their thousands for a week-long beer-and-barbecue binge. Many might be too sozzled to notice things have changed, but that's hardly the point. Hockenheim's one distinguishing characteristic will have been consigned to history. Which is sad.

ACCESS RATING FOR BRITS ★★★★

Easy to get to by air (an hour and a bit from Frankfurt) or road (about five hours from Calais, although we don't recommend driving the wrong way down dual carriageways, a tactic unwittingly tried by veteran F1 correspondent Tony Dodgins this year). Usually unpleasantly humid – but the beer's good

STARTING GRID

6 Montoya
1m38.117s

5 R Schumacher
1m38.136s

3 Hakkinen
1m38.811s

1 M Schumacher
1m38.941s

4 Coulthard
1m39.574s

2 Barrichello
1m39.682s

16 Heidfeld
1m39.921s

17 Raikkonen
1m40.072s

19 de la Rosa
1m40.265s

12 Trulli
1m40.322s

18 Irvine
1m40.371s

10 Villeneuve
1m40.437s

9 Panis
1m40.610s

22 Alesi
1m40.724s

11 Zonta
1m41.174s

23 Burti
1m41.213s

7 Fisichella
1m41.299s

8 Button
1m41.438s

15 Bernoldi
1m41.668s

14 Verstappen
1m41.870s

21 Alonso
1m41.913s

20 Marques
1m42.716s

July 29 2001
HOCKENHEIM-RING, NEAR HEIDELBERG
CIRCUIT LENGTH: 4.241miles / 6.825km

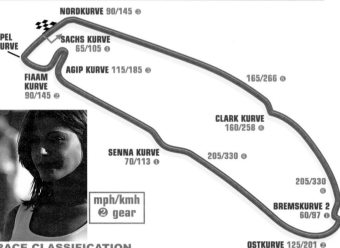

NORDKURVE 90/145 ③
OPEL KURVE
SACHS KURVE 65/105 ①
AGIP KURVE 115/185 ③
FIAAM KURVE 90/145 ②
165/266 ⑥
CLARK KURVE 160/258 ⑥
SENNA KURVE 70/113 ①
205/330 ⑥
205/330 ⑥
BREMSKURVE 2 60/97 ①
mph/kmh ② gear
OSTKURVE 125/201 ②

RACE CLASSIFICATION

Pos	Driver	Nat	Car	Laps	Time
1	Ralf Schumacher	D	Williams FW23-BMW V10	45	1h18m17.873s
2	Rubens Barrichello	BR	Ferrari F2001-Ferrari V10	45	+46.117s
3	Jacques Villeneuve	CDN	BAR 003-Honda V10	45	+1m02.806s
4	Giancarlo Fisichella	I	Benetton B201-Renault V10	45	+1m03.477s
5	Jenson Button	GB	Benetton B201-Renault V10	45	+1m05.454s
6	Jean Alesi	F	Prost AP04-Acer V10	45	+1m05.950s
7	Olivier Panis	F	BAR 003-Honda V10	45	+1m17.527s
8	Enrique Bernoldi	BR	Arrows A22-Asiatech V10		+1 lap
9	Jos Verstappen	NL	Arrows A22-Asiatech V10		+1 lap
10	Fernando Alonso	E	Minardi PS01-European V10		+1 lap

Retirements	Nat	Car	Laps	Reason
Jarno Trulli	I	Jordan EJ11-Honda V10	34	hydraulic pump
David Coulthard	GB	McLaren MP4-16-Mercedes V10	27	engine
Tarso Marques	BR	Minardi PS01-European V10	26	gearbox
Juan Pablo Montoya	CO	Williams FW23-BMW V10	24	engine
Michael Schumacher	D	Ferrari F2001-Ferrari V10	23	fuel pressure
Luciano Burti	BR	Prost AP04-Acer V10	23	spin
Kimi Raikkonen	FIN	Sauber C20-Petronas V10	16	driveshaft
Eddie Irvine	GB	Jaguar R2-Ford Cosworth V10	16	fuel pressure
Mika Hakkinen	FIN	McLaren MP4-16-Mercedes V10	13	engine
Ricardo Zonta	BR	Jordan EJ11-Honda V10	7	accident damage
Nick Heidfeld	D	Sauber C20-Petronas V10	0	accident
Pedro de la Rosa	E	Jaguar R2-Ford Cosworth V10	0	accident

FASTEST LAP Montoya 1m41.808s lap20 (149.960mph/241.337kmh)

DRIVERS' CHAMPIONSHIP

1	Michael Schumacher	84
2	David Coulthard	47
3	Ralf Schumacher	41
4	Rubens Barrichello	40
5	Mika Hakkinen	19
6	Juan Pablo Montoya	15
7	Jacques Villeneuve	11
8	Nick Heidfeld	10
9	Kimi Raikkonen	9
	Jarno Trulli	9
11	Heinz-Harald Frentzen	6
12	Olivier Panis	5
13	Eddie Irvine	4
	Jean Alesi	4
	Giancarlo Fisichella	4
16	Jenson Button	2
17	Jos Verstappen	1
	Pedro de la Rosa	1

CONSTRUCTORS' CHAMPIONSHIP

1	Ferrari	124
2	McLaren-Mercedes	66
3	Williams-BMW	56
4	Sauber-Petronas	19
5	BAR-Honda	16
6	Jordan-Honda	15
7	Benetton-Renault	6
8	Jaguar-Ford Cosworth	5
9	Prost-Acer	4
10	Arrows-Asiatech	1

MARLBORO MAGYAR NAGYDIJ

VICTORY IN HUNGARY WOULD CEMENT A FOURTH WORLD TITLE FOR MICHAEL SCHUMACHER, BUT PRE-RACE HE CLAIMED TO BE FEELING A LITTLE UNEASY. ER, WHY?

THE FIST CUT IS THE DEEPEST: Schuey celebrates equalling Alain Prost's winning record (right). He also set a new benchmark for the number of times a Ferrari has appeared on a double-page spread in this publication. Above, playing happy families with Barrichello (left) and Jean Todt

IT WAS ABSOLUTE STATISTICAL NIRVANA. MICHAEL
Schumacher's success in Budapest clinched his fourth world title
and brought him level with Alain Prost as the most successful driver
in F1 history, leastways in terms of race wins. This was his 51st –
and it had taken him slightly less than 10 seasons to get there.

The other stat, however, was less impressive, because the 2001
Hungarian GP contained just one proper overtaking manoeuvre.
Thanks to Jordan returnee Jean Alesi for reminding us all about
racing spirit, even if he did only pass Pedro de la Rosa's Jaguar for
the dubious honour of running 12th, on the road, in the opening
stages. Still, neat move.

Actually, there were a couple more manoeuvres, but they don't
really count, because it was only Jenson Button repassing the
Minardis while recovering from a penalty stop for jumping the
start: the Benetton has a fantastic launch control system, but the
young Englishman failed to control when he launched it.

Right, that's about 150 words out of the way. Where am I going
to find another 600 or so?

Oh yes, Schuey. He took pole position for the ninth time this
season and was never seriously challenged. He might be a master
of circuits that test others' fear thresholds (ie Spa), but he is also
blindingly good around the twiddly stuff (ie Budapest).

David Coulthard was his closest rival in qualifying – but being
second on the grid here is more disadvantageous than usual,
because when drivers talk about the "dirty" side of the track, they
really mean dirty. The only form of motor sport dustier than the
Hungarian GP is the Paris-Dakar Rally, and even parts of the
Sahara offer more purchase than DC was able to find, as he

NIGEL MANSELL MIGHT HAVE WON HERE FROM 13TH ON THE GRID IN 1989, BUT THAT WAS A HISTORICAL BLIP. PASSING WAS STRICTLY A THING OF THE PAST

watched Schuey disappear towards the first turn. Worse, Rubens
Barrichello was able to zap past from third on the grid and the
result was settled. Nigel Mansell might have won here from 13th
on the grid in 1989, but that was a historical blip. Passing was
strictly a thing of the past. Besides, remember Thiery Boutsen
holding up Ayrton Senna, of all people, for 77 laps in 1990? The
words "Budapest", "racetrack" and "not" spring readily to mind.

It might have been an uneventful afternoon, but the crowd –
largely German and totally drunk – gave the ecstatic winner the
most raucous reception in the history of grand prix racing.
Michael bounced around a bit then paused to reflect.

"It has been a fantastic weekend," he said. "I didn't have such a
good feeling coming into this race, for whatever reason, but we
got everything done. The title is a bit too much to take in right now,
but the way it has been done makes it so fantastic, because you
can't believe how wonderful the guys are, how much we stick
together, in good times as well as bad. We have such a great crew
– it's their achievement."

Barrichello certainly played his part. He eased off during his
first stint and forced the following Coulthard to do likewise. The

NO ROOM AT THE FINN:
Hakkinen and Raikkonen
find their path into the
first corner blocked by
(from left, above) Schuey
Jnr, Trulli and Heidfeld.
Meanwhile, still at the
first turn (right), the
world's self-proclaimed
"second best driver"
(clue, he's in a Jaguar
that's not on the same
bit of track as the rest)
struggles to convince us
of as much

CAMPAIGN FOR REAL ALESI

You have just sacked one of your own drivers on the grounds of mild underperformance. But there are few obvious replacements.

Time was, when an F1 team strapped for a substitute would simply dip its hand into an unproven talent pool and give a young gun his chance. That's how Jean Alesi (above) came to make his F1 debut for Tyrrell in the 1989 French GP.

At the time he was a front-runner in the FIA F3000 series. That now serves as a grand prix support formula, so it's not easy to pick some young drivers because they tend to be otherwise engaged during GP weekends.

In 1989 Alesi drove for Eddie Jordan Racing, Jordan GP's fore-runner, in F1's feeder formula – and 12 years on the Irishman turned again to his long-standing friend. Alesi might have been 37, but he had to be a better bet than Ricardo Zonta, who previously deputised without distinction for the axed Heinz-Harald Frentzen. Fortunately for Jordan, Alesi was in the throes of leaving Prost GP because of a spat and the Frenchman swiftly signed up.

A conservative choice? Yes, but a reliable one. For all his engaging loopiness, Alesi is the best finisher in the business, bar none. Before rejoining Jordan he was the only driver to have been classified for every race during the 2001 season (although he spent his final two laps in the gravel at the Nürburgring, admittedly).

There is only one picture in the Jordan factory. It hangs on the wall in the canteen. It's quite old and is signed by the driver: "Jean Alesi, 1989." Old flames still flickered and the team was pleased to welcome him back.

SECOND HELPING: Barrichello quits the pits, where he gained an edge on Coulthard

THE WILLIAMS FW23S WEREN'T EXPECTED TO SHINE, PARTLY BECAUSE THE BMW V10 DOESN'T HAVE A CHANCE TO STRETCH ITS LEGS ON THIS GRUBBY TOURNIQUET OF A TRACK

pair swapped places after the first round of pit stops, but DC was unable to make ground on the leader. . . and then slipped back behind Barrichello when they stopped for a second time.

The Williams FW23s weren't expected to shine here, partly because they don't generate the same level of downforce as their rivals, partly because the BMW V10 doesn't really have a chance to stretch its legs on this grubby tourniquet of a track. Still, Ralf Schumacher started fourth and held Mika Hakkinen off for most of the race. McLaren tried to get the Finn ahead by giving him a shorter second stop. The plan was to gain track position, clear off up the road and have enough time to add a splash of fuel late on. Unfortunately Mika emerged still behind Ralf and was thus compelled to follow him before losing ground when he refuelled for the third and final time. The Finn netted fastest lap, however, which proved that the McLaren had been trapped, rather than merely tardy.

Sauber continued to embarrass BAR and Jordan in the world championship for constructors and Nick Heidfeld followed Hakkinen across the line to give the Swiss team another point. It was his latest in a series of fine drives.

His team-mate Kimi Raikkonen and Juan Pablo Montoya (better on quick circuits than tight, technical ones) were next. Eddie Irvine – who had recently claimed in an *Autosport* interview that he was the world's second best driver – went a long way to disproving his own theory by spinning his Jaguar into retirement at the first corner. ■

CITIZEN KEEN

There is a notion that says all Formula One races should take place close the centre of major conurbations (all right, apart from Sao Paulo).

Melbourne? Great event. Montreal? Ditto. And Budapest (actually two cities – Buda and Pest) falls into the same category. The track might be a pit, but the Hungarian capital – all of 20 minutes away by car (watch out for dodgy lorries with unfastened loads on the M3 motorway) – helps soften the blow.

Culturally diverse, architecturally fascinating and bisected by the River Danube, Budapest remains the only city from behind the old Iron Curtain to have staged a world championship grand prix.

Back in 1986, the race's first season, organisers promised F1 that the circus would be able to function as in any other country – although motorhome crews didn't agree, largely because traders understandably limited visitors to the same rations as locals were accustomed to. And a couple of spuds weren't much use when you had to rustle up dinner for 30. . .

Times might have changed, but some parts of Budapest haven't. One café – New York, New York – remains propped up by wooden stilts that have been there since the army tried to enter via the front door in 1968, but forgot to remove their tank first. In 2001 it was closed for renovation, which was sad for habitués. Progress is sometimes desirable, but one hopes a couple of things will remain: the wooden props – and the in-house string quartet that plays everything from Strauss waltzes to the *Match of the Day* theme.

ACCESS RATING FOR BRITS ★★★★
Not as tricky as you might think. Flights are regular and only take a couple of hours. Think of it as going to Germany – but slightly farther and 20 times more fun

STARTING GRID

1 M Schumacher
1m14.059s

4 Coulthard
1m14.860s

2 Barrichello
1m14.953s

5 R Schumacher
1m15.095s

11 Trulli
1m15.394s

3 Hakkinen
1m15.411s

16 Heidfeld
1m15.739s

6 Montoya
1m15.881s

17 Raikkonen
1m15.906s

10 Villeneuve
1m16.212s

9 Panis
1m16.382s

12 Alesi
1m16.471s

19 de la Rosa
1m16.543s

18 Irvine
1m16.607s

7 Fisichella
1m16.632s

22 Frentzen
1m17.196s

8 Button
1m17.535s

21 Alonso
1m17.624s

23 Burti
1m18.238s

15 Bernoldi
1m18.258s

14 Verstappen
1m18.389s

20 Marques
1m19.139s

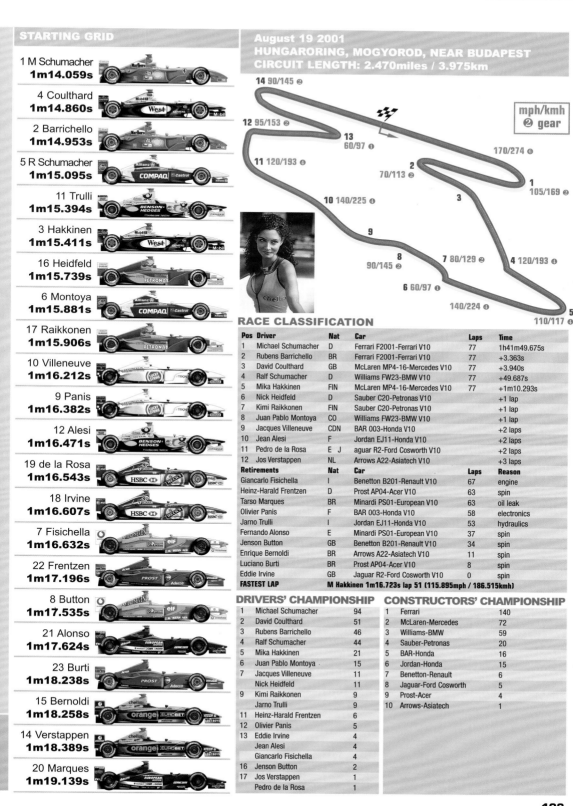

August 19 2001
HUNGARORING, MOGYOROD, NEAR BUDAPEST
CIRCUIT LENGTH: 2.470miles / 3.975km

mph/kmh
❷ gear

RACE CLASSIFICATION

Pos	Driver	Nat	Car	Laps	Time
1	Michael Schumacher	D	Ferrari F2001-Ferrari V10	77	1h41m49.675s
2	Rubens Barrichello	BR	Ferrari F2001-Ferrari V10	77	+3.363s
3	David Coulthard	GB	McLaren MP4-16-Mercedes V10	77	+3.940s
4	Ralf Schumacher	D	Williams FW23-BMW V10	77	+49.687s
5	Mika Hakkinen	FIN	McLaren MP4-16-Mercedes V10	77	+1m10.293s
6	Nick Heidfeld	D	Sauber C20-Petronas V10		+1 lap
7	Kimi Raikkonen	FIN	Sauber C20-Petronas V10		+1 lap
8	Juan Pablo Montoya	CO	Williams FW23-BMW V10		+1 lap
9	Jacques Villeneuve	CDN	BAR 003-Honda V10		+2 laps
10	Jean Alesi	F	Jordan EJ11-Honda V10		+2 laps
11	Pedro de la Rosa	E J	aguar R2-Ford Cosworth V10		+2 laps
12	Jos Verstappen	NL	Arrows A22-Asiatech V10		+3 laps

Retirements	Nat	Car	Laps	Reason
Giancarlo Fisichella	I	Benetton B201-Renault V10	67	engine
Heinz-Harald Frentzen	D	Prost AP04-Acer V10	63	spin
Tarso Marques	BR	Minardi PS01-European V10	63	oil leak
Olivier Panis	F	BAR 003-Honda V10	58	electronics
Jarno Trulli	I	Jordan EJ11-Honda V10	53	hydraulics
Fernando Alonso	E	Minardi PS01-European V10	37	spin
Jenson Button	GB	Benetton B201-Renault V10	34	spin
Enrique Bernoldi	BR	Arrows A22-Asiatech V10	11	spin
Luciano Burti	BR	Prost AP04-Acer V10	8	spin
Eddie Irvine	GB	Jaguar R2-Ford Cosworth V10	0	spin

FASTEST LAP M Hakkinen 1m16.723s lap 51 (115.895mph / 186.515kmh)

DRIVERS' CHAMPIONSHIP

1	Michael Schumacher	94
2	David Coulthard	51
3	Rubens Barrichello	46
4	Ralf Schumacher	44
5	Mika Hakkinen	21
6	Juan Pablo Montoya	15
7	Jacques Villeneuve	11
	Nick Heidfeld	11
9	Kimi Raikkonen	9
	Jarno Trulli	9
11	Heinz-Harald Frentzen	6
12	Olivier Panis	5
13	Eddie Irvine	4
	Jean Alesi	4
	Giancarlo Fisichella	4
16	Jenson Button	2
17	Jos Verstappen	1
	Pedro de la Rosa	1

CONSTRUCTORS' CHAMPIONSHIP

1	Ferrari	140
2	McLaren-Mercedes	72
3	Williams-BMW	59
4	Sauber-Petronas	20
5	BAR-Honda	16
6	Jordan-Honda	15
7	Benetton-Renault	6
8	Jaguar-Ford Cosworth	5
9	Prost-Acer	4
10	Arrows-Asiatech	1

KEN TYRRELL – AN APPRECIATION

THE TEAM THAT BORE HIS NAME LAST WON A RACE IN 1983 AND VANISHED FROM VIEW AT THE END OF THE 1998 SEASON. BUT KEN TYRRELL, WHO DIED ON AUGUST 25 2001, REMAINED A MOTOR RACING LEGEND. TONY DODGINS PAYS TRIBUTE

ROBERT KEN TYRRELL BELONGED to a different era, in the nicest possible way. His word was his bond and his business was done on a handshake.

Ken discovered motor racing almost by accident. Football was his great love, but when his local club organised a day out at Silverstone Ken was smitten. He knew instantly what he wanted to do. At first he fancied himself as a driver and bought himself a share in a Cooper-Norton, which he ran for the first time at Snetterton in 1952.

Tyrrell was running a pair of F2 Coopers by 1958 and drove one himself. A timber merchant by vocation, his emblem was a woodman's axe, hence the nickname "Chopper".

Towards the end of that season a 21-year-old Kiwi, Bruce McLaren, beat Tyrrell at Brands Hatch and Ken decided it was time to concentrate on team management. And Bruce was to play a crucial role in another of Ken's key decisions five years on.

Ken established the Tyrrell Racing Team to run Formula Junior Coopers out of the family timber yard in 1960. One of his early drivers, former bobsleigh racer Henry Taylor, gave the team its first international success with victory in the Prix Monaco Junior. Tyrrell was also the man who gave 1964 world champion John Surtees his first race on four wheels.

Ken's forthright manner and a natural bent towards organisation allowed him to strike up a strong relationship with the late John Cooper. When Cooper injured himself crashing his twin-engined Mini prototype, he turned to Ken to run his grand prix team while he convalesced.

Ken's appetite was whetted but, for '63, it was back to Cooper Formula Juniors and a newly-formed Tyrrell Racing Organisation. A year later, Ken found himself looking for a driver after Timmy Mayer was killed in an accident in Tasmania.

Chatting with the Goodwood circuit boss, Jackie Stewart's name came up. Tyrrell invited the 24-year-old Scot down for a test and arranged for the now well-established McLaren to set a target time. Stewart beat it within three laps. Tyrrell ticked him off for trying too hard. He sent McLaren out again and Bruce went quicker. Jackie beat him again. Ken called a halt while his car still had four corners and signed Jackie immediately. Together they won 16 races that year.

For the next three seasons Ken ran F2 cars for Stewart and began a partnership with the French Matra organisation. Jackie was racing BRMs in F1 and, by the end of '67, Ken knew he was ready to move up. He had also witnessed the F1 debut of the Cosworth DFV engine in the back of Jim Clark's Lotus and did everything he could to put together a Stewart/Matra/Cosworth

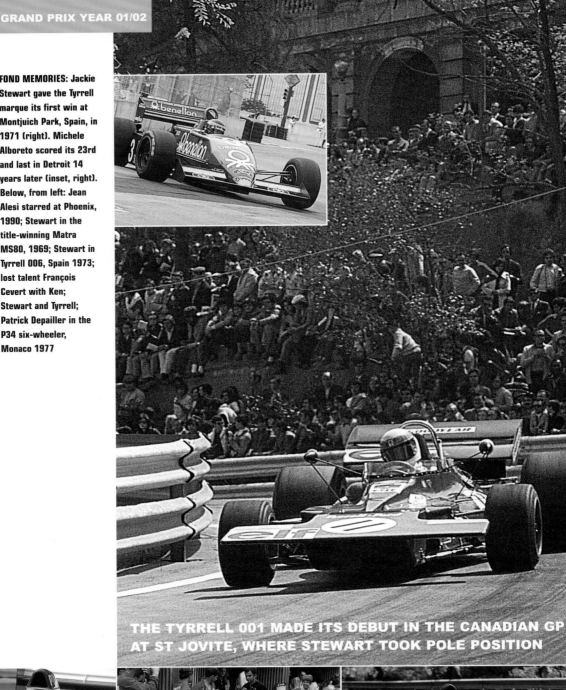

FOND MEMORIES: Jackie Stewart gave the Tyrrell marque its first win at Montjuich Park, Spain, in 1971 (right). Michele Alboreto scored its 23rd and last in Detroit 14 years later (inset, right). Below, from left: Jean Alesi starred at Phoenix, 1990; Stewart in the title-winning Matra MS80, 1969; Stewart in Tyrrell 006, Spain 1973; lost talent François Cevert with Ken; Stewart and Tyrrell; Patrick Depailler in the P34 six-wheeler, Monaco 1977

THE TYRRELL 001 MADE ITS DEBUT IN THE CANADIAN GP AT ST JOVITE, WHERE STEWART TOOK POLE POSITION

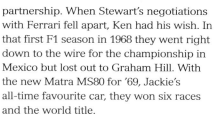

partnership. When Stewart's negotiations with Ferrari fell apart, Ken had his wish. In that first F1 season in 1968 they went right down to the wire for the championship in Mexico but lost out to Graham Hill. With the new Matra MS80 for '69, Jackie's all-time favourite car, they won six races and the world title.

Ken was dragged into the world of F1 construction out of expediency rather than any great desire. Simca took over Matra in '69 and so the Matra-Ford partnership was on borrowed time. Ken was forced to turn to one of new company March's unproven chassis for his reigning world champion. He was not happy that the fledgling organisation planned to have five cars on the grid for the first race at Kyalami, South Africa.

By chance, Ken bumped into engineer Derek Gardner at Heathrow while the latter was working at Ferguson Research on a planned four-wheel-drive system for Matra. During the flight to Paris, Gardner mentioned he was thinking of going freelance. Ken commissioned him to build an F1 car, to be ready by the following August's Oulton Park Gold Cup. It was perhaps F1's best-kept secret of all time.

The Tyrrell 001 made its GP debut in Canada, at St Jovite, where Stewart took pole position. The new constructor's first win came with chassis 003 at Barcelona in '71 and Stewart went on to win his second world title. Charismatic Frenchman François Cevert was keen to learn from "the maestro" and scored his lone GP win that same season at Watkins Glen.

Two years later, Cevert was killed in a practice accident at the same track in what was to have been Stewart's 100th and final grand prix. It signalled a desperately sad end to a three-year period that produced 16 grand prix wins, two drivers titles for Stewart (1971 and 1973) and a constructors' title in that first season for Ken.

When Stewart retired at the end of '73 he paid generous tribute to Tyrrell, saying: "Ken has shaped my personality in racing." But it was a symbiotic relationship and Tyrrell never again experienced the heights of those early years. There was the memorable Project 34 six-wheeler and there were grand prix wins for Jody Scheckter, Patrick Depailler and Michele Alboreto, but never the hint of a repeat of that constructors' championship.

Ultimately, statistics are not what Ken Tyrrell was about. He was a personality, a character. He ran his team with the same unflinching personal and moral values right up until the day, in 1997, when he took the decision to sell his place on the grid to the fledgling British American Racing team. Like Frank Williams and Ron Dennis, he was a racer – one of the old school. Occasionally the phone would ring and there would be no introduction, just the resonant voice, the same conviction and the details of some wager Ken was offering based on one of his hunches.

Still globetrotting in his seventies, usually with wife Norah by his side, he was one of life's enthusiasts, never far away from the latest developments at Spurs or with test cricket. A sportsman and a gentleman, the racing world is a poorer place for his loss. ■

MICHAEL SCHUMACHER HAD THE FORTUNE TO ARRIVE ON THE PLANET BLESSED WITH EXTRAORDINARY NATURAL GIFTS – BUT HE WASN'T THE LUCKIEST DRIVER AT SPA, DESPITE HIS RECORD-BREAKING PERFORMANCE

FOSTER'S BELGIAN GRAND PRIX

RALF GARNET: Schuey Jnr made a jewel of a start (right) after his pole-sitting team-mate was sent to the back of the class, but his brother (above) was past within a few seconds. From that moment, his record-breaking 52nd F1 win was never in doubt

IT WAS POISED TO BE A THRILLER. THE TWO WILLIAMS-
BMWs nestled on the front row after a canny qualifying performance. Juan Pablo Montoya and Ralf Schumacher opted for Michelin slicks on a damp, but drying, track and left even Schuey Snr trailing in their wake.

Chasing a epoch-making 52nd grand prix win at the circuit where he had made a spectacular F1 debut 10 years beforehand, he was miles behind the Williams pair – although he had managed only one lap on slicks to their two, which exaggerated the disparity. And while Ralf's lap looked good, Montoya's was simply stunning. Almost nine-tenths up on his team-mate and more than 10mph faster through the man-or-mouse challenge that is Eau Rouge, it was the Colombian at his fearless best.

And then he stalled on the grid.

Any hope that Schuey Jnr might make a race of it vanished within 20 seconds of the start when Michael breezed past on the climb to Les Combes as though his brother were still on foot. BMW's V10 might have a lot of grunt, but the Williams FW23 was running a fair amount of wing and was no match in race trim for the sleeker Ferrari. Thereafter Schuey was untroubled, other than by some of the chaos he saw around him. Small wonder that he adores Spa-Francorchamps: he made his first F1 start here, scored his first grand prix victory here in 1992 and this was his 52nd such triumph, which made him the most successful driver in F1 history in terms of race victories.

MICHAEL BREEZED PAST ON THE RUN TO LES COMBES AS THOUGH HIS BROTHER WERE STILL ON FOOT

It put him one clear of Alain Prost, but the modern-day team owner had more pressing concerns in Belgium. His weekend had started brightly enough, when Heinz-Harald Frentzen qualified an improbable fourth after being one of the few to profit from running slicks at the end of the session. Not for the first time in the launch control era, however, he got his buttons in a muddle and stalled, which caused the original start to be aborted and dropped him to the tail of the field, where Montoya would shortly join him.

Once they were up and running, the race lasted just four laps before Frentzen's team-mate Luciano Burti brushed wheels with Eddie Irvine's Jaguar as they disputed 15th place through the 185mph left-hander at Blanchimont. Unusually in contemporary F1, the consequences were sufficiently alarming for the race to be red-flagged rather than merely neutralised behind the Safety Car (see sidebar, right).

More than 40 minutes later the race restarted – in some confusion. Previously in such situations, the result has been taken as an aggregate of two parts either side of a stoppage, but the rules were changed at the beginning of the season so that drivers would be classified in the order that they passed the chequered flag (which is easier to follow for TV punters). The FIA, which makes the rules, appeared to have forgotten this and initially said the first four laps would be added to the final 36 to determine a result, but eventually someone remembered what the latest

RENAULT BRIO: Fisichella (above) was on top form and made Coulthard (right) work hard for his keep. Still, better than following an Arrows, David. Far right, Barrichello wonders what makes Schuey so good. For a start, Rubens, he tends not to clump into the barriers at the Bus Stop chicane. Below right, Heidfeld and Montoya gang up on de la Rosa at the restart. The Sauber and the Jag fell to bits as a result

THE SCHOOL OF HARD KNOCKS

It is rare that a circuit falls wholly silent during the course of a grand prix. When it happens, you don't need to be told that something is awry. You can feel it.

There had been several sizeable accidents at Spa before the race, but none with serious consequences. When Luciano Burti and Eddie Irvine collided at Blanchimont on lap four, however, the outcome looked terrifying.

Irvine careered off the road and struck the barriers a harsh but glancing blow. His car was trashed, but he hopped out unharmed. Burti, his front wing ripped away by the initial impact, simply ploughed head on into the tyre-lined guardrail at barely abated speed – 173mph according to the telemetry. The barriers, fortunately, are at a relatively shallow angle at that point, but Burti – who had survived a horrifying startline crash in Hockenheim only two races earlier, remember – was buried deep beneath a hefty pile of tyres that Irvine and the marshals had some difficulty removing.

The situation initially looked grave, but the Brazilian was removed relatively swiftly from the wreck. He was no more than severely bruised and shaken, although he was to spend the next few days under observation in a Liège hospital.

Some observers felt Irvine should have been severely punished for moving across when Burti had poked his Prost's nose inside the Jaguar. The Ulsterman claimed he hadn't expected Burti to attempt a pass at that point – and others concurred that it had been an improbably brave lunge on the Brazilian's part. The stewards decreed it to be just a racing incident and no further action was taken.

Although bruised and battered, Luciano's spirit was intact. When close pal Rubens Barrichello paid him a visit, the first thing Burti is alleged to have told him is that he was itching to be released in order to thump Irvine.

AGE SHALL NOT WITHER: Frentzen (left) lined up fourth; Alesi finished sixth

FISICHELLA WAS INSPIRED IN THE PREVIOUSLY RECALCITRANT BENETTON AND MADE AWESOME STARTS TO BOTH PARTS OF THE RACE

regulations specify. History will record that the first few laps of the race never happened, although Burti might beg to differ.

The one thing that was abundantly clear was Michael's continued superiority. He thought Ralf might give him a hard time on the run to La Source at the restart – except that the Williams was still up on jacks because the team had been fiddling around with the rear wing and hadn't had time to complete the job.

But the new record-holder wasn't the only star of the race. Giancarlo Fisichella was inspired in the previously recalcitrant Benetton and made awesome starts to both parts of the race. The second time he vaulted from sixth to second and proceeded to hold off David Coulthard's McLaren for an improbably long time. The Scot eventually made it past, ironically aided when Fisichella lost a bit of momentum as they came up to lap Coulthard's Monaco nemesis, Enrique Bernoldi.

There were two McLarens in the race, although there might as well not have been. Bundled wide at the restart, Mika Hakkinen looked thoroughly disinterested for the rest of the afternoon and tooled home fourth. Jarno Trulli should have been fifth for Jordan, but his engine blew and prompted him to start head-banging the tyre wall in frustration, which was odd.

Rubens Barrichello was thus next across the line, despite being delayed when he knocked off his front wing at the chicane, and Jean Alesi scored his first point for Jordan since September 1989 (when the team was still in Formula 3000) with a spirited late-race defence to fend off the recovering Schuey Jnr. Montoya? He only had time to make modest progress before his engine blew.

Smiling once he learned that Burti was relatively unscathed, the winner said: "Breaking records is nice, but statistics don't bother me too much. They are something to reflect on later, when I sit in a chair with a cigar and a beer."

For his rivals, that can't come soon enough. ∎

ROAD TO JOY

Earlier in the season a Canadian journalist asked Michael Schumacher why he didn't like Montreal. The German raised his eyes and shook his head in exasperation.

"Look," he said, "I never told anyone I don't like Montreal. Spa is my favourite circuit, that's all. It doesn't mean I don't enjoy the others."

With that, he spoke for the whole field.

Every driver adores Spa. Sure, it can bite if you get it wrong – as it did several times in 2001. Luciano Burti apart, David Coulthard, Juan Pablo Montoya, Fernando Alonso and Mark Webber (in Saturday afternoon's Formula 3000 race) all had accidents that ranged from sizeable to colossal. Webber suffered a swollen ankle and limped away; the others walked.

Other circuits have challenging, high-speed corners – but none has such a concentration as Spa. Coming two weeks after the arduous labyrinth that is the Hungaroring, Spa is a breath of fresh air (fresh being the operative word, as temperatures were down to about 3degC).

The track is sufficiently splendid that you can forgive its customarily crap weather. This year Saturday morning's free practice had to be halved because conditions were too foggy for the medical helicopter to fly.

And its atmosphere is always effervescent. Most of Germany pours across the border to set up camp in the surrounding forest. And so does about half of Holland. Come rain, shine or flash flood, they spend the weekend cheerfully sizzling sausages and sozzling beer. Even, in the Germans' case, when their soccer team is being stuffed 5-1.

ACCESS RATING FOR BRITS ★★★★★
A breeze. Less than three hours from Calais by car (but be wary of the Brussels ring road, which is utterly rubbish). For the peckish, many Belgian motorway rest halts have mobile catering units selling chips sloshed with mayonnaise. Strangely, however, you do see some thin Belgians

STARTING GRID

6 Montoya
1m52.072s

5 R Schumacher
1m52.959s

1 M Schumacher
1m54.685s

22 Frentzen
1m55.233s

2 Barrichello
1m56.116s

10 Villeneuve
1m57.038s

3 Hakkinen
1m57.043s

7 Fisichella
1m57.668s

4 Coulthard
1m58.008s

19 de la Rosa
1m58.519s

9 Panis
1m58.838s

17 Raikkonen
1m59.050s

12 Alesi
1m59.128s

16 Heidfeld
1m59.302s

8 Button
1m59.587s

11 Trulli
1m59.647s

18 Irvine
1m59.689s

23 Burti
1m59.900s

14 Verstappen
2m2.039s

21 Alonso
2m2.594s

15 Bernoldi
2m3.048s

20 Marques
2m4.204s

September 2 2001
CIRCUIT DE SPA-FRANCORCHAMPS, STAVELOT
CIRCUIT LENGTH: 4.330miles / 6.968km

LA SOURCE 45/72 ➊
EAU ROUGE 180/290 ➏
RAIDILLON 180/290 ➏
'BUS STOP' CHICANE 55/89 ➋
KEMMEL
BLANCHIMONT 190/306 ➎
205/330 ➏
POUHON 145/233 ➍
LES COMBES 85/137 ➌
STAVELOT 150/241 ➍
FAGNES 105/169 ➌
MALMÉDY 100/161 ➋
RIVAGE 70/113 ➋

mph/kmh ➋ gear

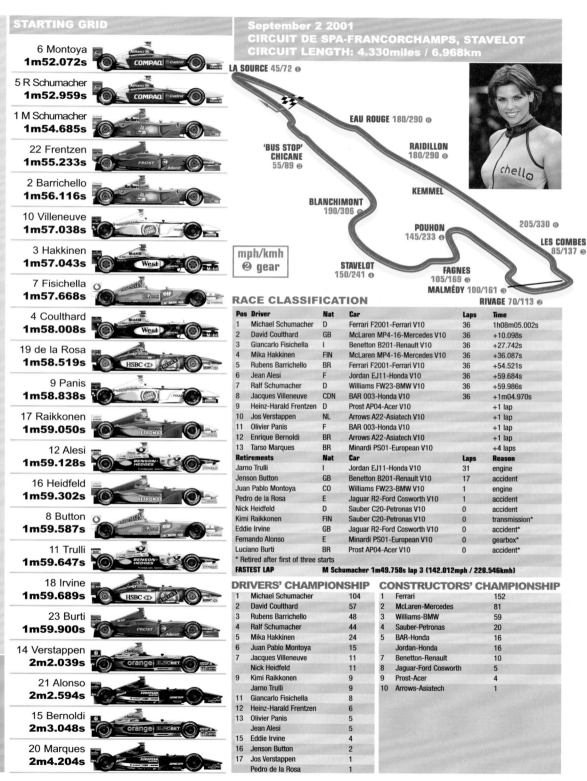

RACE CLASSIFICATION

Pos	Driver	Nat	Car	Laps	Time
1	Michael Schumacher	D	Ferrari F2001-Ferrari V10	36	1h08m05.002s
2	David Coulthard	GB	McLaren MP4-16-Mercedes V10	36	+10.098s
3	Giancarlo Fisichella	I	Benetton B201-Renault V10	36	+27.742s
4	Mika Hakkinen	FIN	McLaren MP4-16-Mercedes V10	36	+36.087s
5	Rubens Barrichello	BR	Ferrari F2001-Ferrari V10	36	+54.521s
6	Jean Alesi	F	Jordan EJ11-Honda V10	36	+59.684s
7	Ralf Schumacher	D	Williams FW23-BMW V10	36	+59.986s
8	Jacques Villeneuve	CDN	BAR 003-Honda V10	36	+1m04.970s
9	Heinz-Harald Frentzen	D	Prost AP04-Acer V10		+1 lap
10	Jos Verstappen	NL	Arrows A22-Asiatech V10		+1 lap
11	Olivier Panis	F	BAR 003-Honda V10		+1 lap
12	Enrique Bernoldi	BR	Arrows A22-Asiatech V10		+1 lap
13	Tarso Marques	BR	Minardi PS01-European V10		+4 laps
Retirements		**Nat**	**Car**	**Laps**	**Reason**
	Jarno Trulli	I	Jordan EJ11-Honda V10	31	engine
	Jenson Button	GB	Benetton B201-Renault V10	17	accident
	Juan Pablo Montoya	CO	Williams FW23-BMW V10	1	engine
	Pedro de la Rosa	E	Jaguar R2-Ford Cosworth V10	1	accident
	Nick Heidfeld	D	Sauber C20-Petronas V10	0	accident
	Kimi Raikkonen	FIN	Sauber C20-Petronas V10	0	transmission*
	Eddie Irvine	GB	Jaguar R2-Ford Cosworth V10	0	accident*
	Fernando Alonso	E	Minardi PS01-European V10	0	gearbox*
	Luciano Burti	BR	Prost AP04-Acer V10	0	accident*

* Retired after first of three starts

FASTEST LAP M Schumacher 1m49.758s lap 3 (142.012mph / 228.546kmh)

DRIVERS' CHAMPIONSHIP

1	Michael Schumacher	104
2	David Coulthard	57
3	Rubens Barrichello	48
4	Ralf Schumacher	44
5	Mika Hakkinen	24
6	Juan Pablo Montoya	15
7	Jacques Villeneuve	11
	Nick Heidfeld	11
9	Kimi Raikkonen	9
	Jarno Trulli	9
11	Giancarlo Fisichella	8
12	Heinz-Harald Frentzen	6
13	Olivier Panis	5
	Jean Alesi	5
15	Eddie Irvine	4
16	Jenson Button	2
17	Jos Verstappen	1
	Pedro de la Rosa	1

CONSTRUCTORS' CHAMPIONSHIP

1	Ferrari	152
2	McLaren-Mercedes	81
3	Williams-BMW	59
4	Sauber-Petronas	20
5	BAR-Honda	16
	Jordan-Honda	16
7	Benetton-Renault	10
8	Jaguar-Ford Cosworth	5
9	Prost-Acer	4
10	Arrows-Asiatech	1

GROOMED WITH A VIEW

LAST YEAR WE SAID THE ROAD TO FORMULA ONE WAS BECOMING TOUGHER FOR YOUNG DRIVERS. NOW EVERYBODY WANTS ONE. WELL, EXCEPT ONE TALL, TALENTED ONE, APPARENTLY. HERE, IN ALPHABETICAL ORDER, IS OUR GUIDE TO SOME OF THE MOST PROMISING RISING STARS OF THE PAST 12 MONTHS

FELIPE MASSA

2001 FORM Formula Renault Eurocup champ graduated to Italy-based Euro F3000 series and won it at a canter. Unlike some of the leading FIA F3000 racers, however, he's breezing straight into F1

F1 POTENTIAL Sauber thinks it has next season's Kimi Raikkonen under lock and key. Testing performances suggest this might be a fair assessment

GIORGIO PANTANO

2001 FORM Found it tough to adapt to FIA F3000, but it's not easy when you were racing karts only 18 months earlier. Had things sussed by the end of the season. One of several potential champs in the series for 2002

F1 POTENTIAL Pretty good – and Italy needs all the help it can get as it hasn't had a world champ since 1953

ANTONIO PIZZONIA

2001 FORM Former British F3 champ quickly adapted to FIA F3000 and scored a brilliant win at Hockenheim. Racecraft had a couple of rough edges, especially when he tried to drive Pantano off the track at Monza, but he's massively quick and learns fast too.

F1 POTENTIAL Pace in a Williams bodes well – as does his particularly fast name

TAKUMA SATO

2001 FORM The first Japanese driver to win an F3 title outside his own country (although Ryo Fukuda and Toshihiro Kaneishi swiftly followed, in France and Germany). Dominated in Britain, despite pressure that came from being overwhelming favourite. Calm, bright and articulate – possibly Japan's best prospect yet

F1 POTENTIAL Pretty good, as Jordan has already signed him to a two-year race deal

RICARDO SPERAFICO

2001 FORM Stepped up to the FIA F3000 series and swiftly settled in as a fast, consistent and thoughtful racer. Not always as quick as team-mate Antonio Pizzonia (see left), but had a more measured approach that earned him points rather than bills for accident damage. His lone victory at Spa was magnificent

F1 POTENTIAL Too early to judge, but he has impressed Williams in testing

MARK WEBBER

2001 FORM Justin Wilson's closest rival in FIA F3000 series. Three wins is usually the foundation of a title-winning season, except when you are up against an awesomely consistent opponent. Did a great job testing F1 for Benetton Renault, though, and sometimes covered three GP distances in as many days

F1 POTENTIAL Huge – quick and an Australian driver would be an asset to the sport commercially

JUSTIN WILSON

2001 FORM Broke all FIA F3000 records. Finished in the top six 11 times in 12 races – and was on the podium in 10 of those. Beat Juan Pablo Montoya's record for number of points scored in a season. Then largely overlooked by F1 teams, despite showing great pace in a Jordan. His 6ft 3in frame puts people off, but if you are fast enough, you are surely short enough?

F1 POTENTIAL As big as he is, given the chance. ■

WHERE ARE THEY NOW?

HOW SOME OF OUR PREVIOUS TIPS HAVE FARED

FERNANDO ALONSO (2000)
– was an F3000 star, now an F1 star (yes, even in a Minardi). Hit

WESTLEY BARBER (1999)
– was in F3, now in, er, Formula Ford. Miss

SÈBASTIEN BOURDAIS (2000)
– was an F3000 ace, remains so. Static

LUCIANO BURTI (1999)
– F3 star went on to be axed by Jaguar, then crashed a lot with Prost. Miss

JENSON BUTTON (1999)
– was in F3, now owns a yacht. Hit

JONATHAN COCHET (2000)
– French F3 champ ran out of dosh; in a rut. Static

PETER DUMBRECK (1999)
– swapped promising single-seater career for life in Germany's DTM. Well paid, but. . . Miss

DARIO FRANCHITTI (1999)
– was a Champ Car ace, still is. Hit

MARC HYNES (1999)
– beat Button to British F3 crown, then vanished. Miss

NICK HEIDFELD (1999)
– former F3000 champ's reputation restored after a great season with Sauber. Hit

BRUNO JUNQUEIRA (1999)
– was an F3000 ace, now Champ Car front-runner. Hit

DARREN MANNING (1999)
– went from F3 glory to F3000 midfield; still there. Static

NICOLAS MINASSIAN (1999)
– was an F3000 ace, tried to be a Champ Car front-runner but got the sack. Miss

FRANCK MONTAGNY (1999)
– F3000 front-runner became a winner, but only in Formula Nissan. Static

JUAN PABLO MONTOYA (1999)
– was a trainee deity, now fully fledged. Hit

KIMI RAIKKONEN (2000)
– told you. We even predicted that McLaren would nick him. Hit

STÈPHANE SARRAZIN (1999)
– was an F3000 race winner and turned out once in F1 for Minardi, but currently on the sidelines. Miss

TOMAS SCHECKTER (2000)
– from F3 spotlight to relative obscurity, via Jag test deal and a dalliance with a hooker. Has the ability to bounce back. Static

GRAN PREMIO CAMPARI D'ITALIA

MONTOYA FINALLY BREAKS HIS DUCK AND IT SHOULD HAVE BEEN A CHAMPAGNE MOMENT – BUT NO ONE FELT LIKE SPRAYING THE BUBBLY WHILE THE WORLD OUTSIDE WAS THREATENING TO TEAR ITSELF APART. SMALL WONDER MONZA WAS SUBDUED

EYE BROWSE: Montoya surveys the monitors (right). Marshals pay their respects (above) in the wake of terrorist attacks in the United States

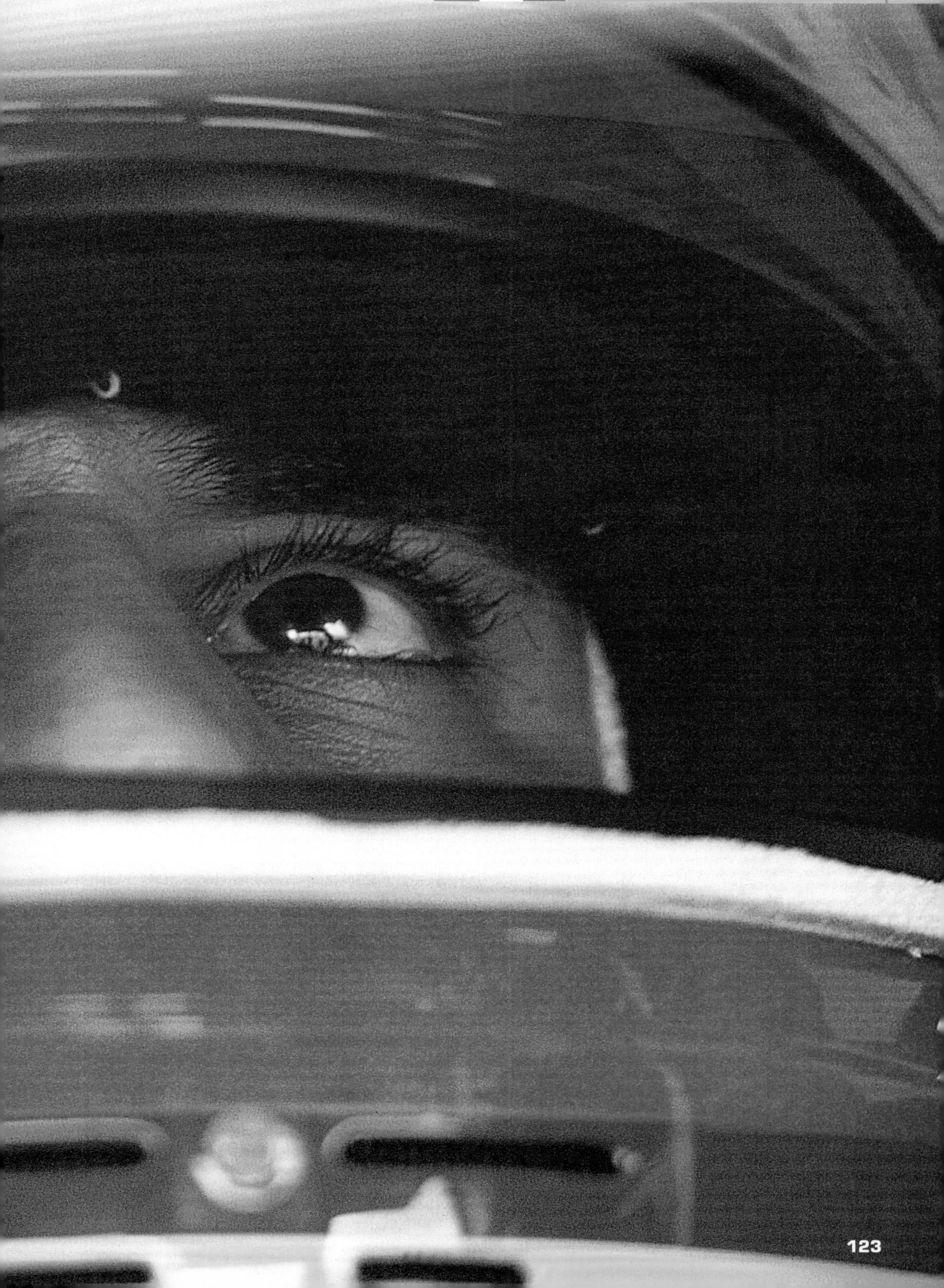

FOR THE FIRST TIME IN HIS FORMULA ONE CAREER, Michael Schumacher gave the impression that he really didn't want to play.

Following appalling terrorist atrocities in the United States three days before cars were due to start practising for the Italian Grand Prix, the world champion consistently questioned if the race should be taking place at all. "You have to ask whether it is right to put on an event like this at such a time," he said. There were many who supported his view, but once the FIA gave the event the green light, most drivers simply turned their minds from the outside world as best as they could and got on with the job.

Schuey, however, was almost invisible – and his mood wasn't helped when former F1 racer Alessandro Zanardi was very seriously injured while taking part in a Champ Car event in Germany during the weekend. Fearing that some kind of cataclysm was about to strike F1, he campaigned on race morning for drivers not to overtake at the first two corners on the opening lap, to avoid a possible repeat of the previous year's pile-up, when flying debris struck and killed a marshal. The two supporting events on the programme, for the FIA Formula 3000 series and Porsche Supercup, had both been marked by spectacular first-lap accidents, fortunately without injury.

BAR driver Jacques Villeneuve was the only dissenting voice: he was here, he said, to race, and that's what he intended to do. Team

TRULLI DEEPLY MADDENED: Jarno spins into retirement (top) after some first-corner GBH from Button, who arrived at the first turn about 140mph faster than anyone else. Good launch control system, though. Raikkonen and someone else with lots of Ks and Ns in his name discuss the price of vodka in Helsinki (possibly, centre left). Schuey wasn't in the mood for a fight all weekend (centre right). Montoya prepares to give his dad a 57th birthday to remember as he sprints away (right) from the Ferraris (decal-free and black-nosed, out of respect for America) at the start

THE FUMBLE COST BARRICHELLO SIX SECONDS: HE LOST THE RACE BY ABOUT FIVE. WITHOUT THE BLUNDER IT WOULD HAVE BEEN MIGHTY CLOSE

managers, too, made it clear to drivers that they expected nothing less and, eventually, the start went ahead as planned.

Perhaps, on a normal day, Michael Schumacher on a two-stop strategy would have won the Italian GP. Ferrari opted to stop twice in order to push the lightning-fast Williams-BMWs of Juan Pablo Montoya and Ralf Schumacher as hard as possible. Montoya qualified on pole – but his BMW's durability was suspect, and on a heavier fuel load his tyres were ripe for a roasting if Ferrari could exert sufficient pressure.

Rubens Barrichello almost did. The Brazilian appeared to be having his best race ever for Ferrari, but with Schuey so subdued it was hard to gauge the car's true potential. Montoya led the early stages, but a mistake at the chicane on the ninth lap allowed Barrichello to pounce. The nimble Ferrari streaked away – but a slow first pit stop was to compromise his chances. Schuey had pitted on lap 18, but by the time Rubens arrived next time around the fuel rig wasn't quite ready. The fumble cost him six seconds; he lost the race by about five. True, Montoya backed off during the last couple of laps – but without Ferrari's pit blunder it would have been mighty close.

No one was about to deny Montoya's right to victory, however. The stocky Colombian – his nation's first-ever GP winner – had come close on several occasions earlier in the season – and his delight was palpable. "It feels fantastic," he said. "People seemed

ACTION NATIONS

Nobody was quite sure when two countries had last simultaneously been represented for the first time in a grand prix. (Answers on a postcard, please, because I can't be bothered looking it up.)

Tomas Enge, from the Czech Republic, made his F1 debut at Monza with Prost, as stand-in for the injured Luciano Burti. Malaysian Alex Yoong joined European Minardi, to replace professional backmarker Tarso Marques.

Enge, three times a race winner in the FIA F3000 series, acquitted himself well. Every time he got in the car, he made progress – so much so, that he set his fastest race lap right at the end. Two seconds slower than team-mate Heinz-Harald Frentzen in qualifying, he was but 0.25s adrift in terms of race pace.

As a child, Tomas was unable to watch his ex-touring car driver father Bratislav in action, because the pre-1989 communist regime didn't allow families to travel en masse. But times have long since changed in Prague – and Enge Snr was looking on proudly when Tomas crossed the line in 12th place.

"I was only really able to watch F1 on TV after about 1990," Enge said, "but I never dreamed I would ever get here. At the time it felt like another world, as far away as the moon."

Yoong, who makes up in Malaysian ringgits (the local currency, not a cheese-and-onion flavour snack) what he lacks in pedigree, fared better than had been predicted (ie he qualified within the mandatory 107 per cent of the pole position time). That was no mean feat, given that he was deprived of track time on Friday morning, because of an electrical failure, and Saturday, because of persistent gearbox trouble.

He had two spins in the race. One happened directly in front of Montoya and Schuey Snr, just as Yoong was about to be lapped. The second put him in the gravel for good. Perhaps the most telling statistic, however, was that his best lap was almost three seconds slower than that of his team-mate, Fernando Alonso.

A SPANIARD IN THE WORKS: de la Rosa (above) raced well after outqualifying Jaguar team-mate Irvine for the fifth straight race. Wrong (right): Hakkinen made a hash of his final qualifying run

DE LA ROSA DID A STERLING JOB FOR JAGUAR, RUNNING IN THE TOP SIX FROM THE START – AND STAYING THERE AFTER A BEAUTIFULLY JUDGED LONG FIRST STINT

to be expecting a lot from me, but I never assumed I would win in my first season. I knew I had a lot to learn."

The second Williams of Schuey Jnr followed Barrichello across the line, while Michael trailed home anonymously in fourth. We saw about five seconds of the real thing, shortly after the start, when he gunned past his brother. But after the final pit stop he emerged behind Ralf – and remained there.

Pedro de la Rosa did a sterling job for Jaguar, running in the top six from the start – and staying there after a beautifully judged long first stint. His fifth place gave Jaguar only its third points finish of the campaign. The BARs were hugely off the pace until race time, when others' problems allowed Villeneuve to work his way through the field to claim the final point.

Among those whose chances were scuppered, fifth-fastest qualifier Jarno Trulli was rammed off at the first corner (Jenson Button – guilty as charged) and the on-form Nick Heidfeld started the spare Sauber from the pits because of a hydraulic leak. Stuck in traffic, he was unable to climb beyond 11th by the end.

The McLarens? Not mentioned so far because they were useless. David Coulthard was running fifth when his engine blew; Mika Hakkinen announced during the weekend that he was to take a break from F1 at the end of the season. As far as most observers were concerned, however, he appeared to have been doing this for some time. ■

SCARLET FEVER

Monza is Europe's oldest active racetrack. Built in 1922 (they started in May and the first race took place in September, which is a bit sharper than the Italian construction industry tends to be nowadays), it lies at the heart of an expansive royal park that forms one of the main features in the town of Monza.

Many view Monza as the spiritual home of European motor racing. Others regard it as a dump where you are more than likely to have bags nicked from the boot of your hire car.

The second faction might have a point, particularly with a view to car security, but nowhere else has Monza's character, which is topped off nicely by fans festooned in bright scarlet Ferrari apparel. Fragments of the old, banked circuit (inactive for many years) remain, and parts of that are barely any more shambling than some of the current infrastructure, but that's what makes Monza special. You can't just replace the current pit buildings with an antiseptic new complex, because the park's trees are sacrosanct and there isn't space for renovation without chopping a few of them down.

Given that this is Italy, and that every access point is manned by about 10 times more stewards than is strictly necessary, it ought to be chaotic. But it isn't. They empty the whole track in about half the time it traditionally takes Silverstone to clear a couple of car parks. The Italians like to refer to Monza as their temple of speed. It is also, however, a shrine to fine food and atmosphere. There is no better racing weekend on the calendar.

ACCESS RATING FOR BRITS *****

Easy. Nearby Milan has two airports (Linate is nearer than Malpensa, and also less crowded) and there are several zillion flights per day. Failing that, it is accessible on the train. Other alternatives include driving (about 11 hours from Calais), hitching or walking (set off about February). Just go, basically

STARTING GRID

6 Montoya
1m22.216s

2 Barrichello
1m22.528s

1 M Schumacher
1m22.624s

5 R Schumacher
1m22.841s

11 Trulli
1m23.126s

4 Coulthard
1m23.148s

3 Hakkinen
1m23.394s

16 Heidfeld
1m23.417s

17 Raikkonen
1m23.595s

19 de la Rosa
1m23.693s

8 Button
1m23.892s

22 Frentzen
1m23.943s

18 Irvine
1m24.031s

7 Fisichella
1m24.090s

10 Villeneuve
1m24.164s

12 Alesi
1m24.198s

9 Panis
1m24.677s

15 Bernoldi
1m25.444s

14 Verstappen
1m25.511s

23 Enge
1m26.039s

21 Alonso
1m26.218s

20 Yoong
1m27.463s

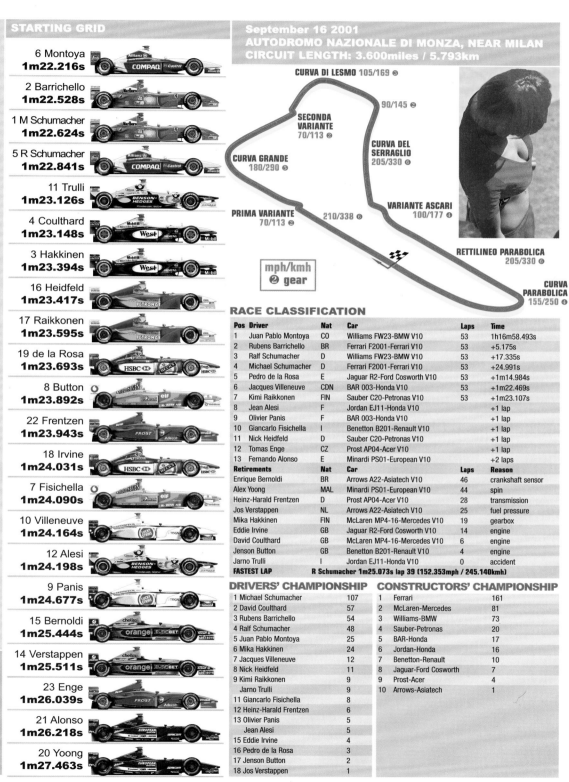

September 16 2001
AUTODROMO NAZIONALE DI MONZA, NEAR MILAN
CIRCUIT LENGTH: 3.600miles / 5.793km

CURVA DI LESMO 105/169 ③

90/145 ②

SECONDA
VARIANTE
70/113 ②

CURVA DEL
SERRAGLIO
205/330 ⑥

CURVA GRANDE
180/290 ⑤

PRIMA VARIANTE
70/113 ②

210/338 ⑥

VARIANTE ASCARI
100/177 ②

RETTILINEO PARABOLICA
205/330 ⑥

mph/kmh
❷ gear

CURVA
PARABOLICA
155/250 ②

RACE CLASSIFICATION

Pos	Driver	Nat	Car	Laps	Time
1	Juan Pablo Montoya	CO	Williams FW23-BMW V10	53	1h16m58.493s
2	Rubens Barrichello	BR	Ferrari F2001-Ferrari V10	53	+5.175s
3	Ralf Schumacher	D	Williams FW23-BMW V10	53	+17.335s
4	Michael Schumacher	D	Ferrari F2001-Ferrari V10	53	+24.991s
5	Pedro de la Rosa	E	Jaguar R2-Ford Cosworth V10	53	+1m14.984s
6	Jacques Villeneuve	CDN	BAR 003-Honda V10	53	+1m22.469s
7	Kimi Raikkonen	FIN	Sauber C20-Petronas V10	53	+1m23.107s
8	Jean Alesi	F	Jordan EJ11-Honda V10		+1 lap
9	Olivier Panis	F	BAR 003-Honda V10		+1 lap
10	Giancarlo Fisichella	I	Benetton B201-Renault V10		+1 lap
11	Nick Heidfeld	D	Sauber C20-Petronas V10		+1 lap
12	Tomas Enge	CZ	Prost AP04-Acer V10		+1 lap
13	Fernando Alonso	E	Minardi PS01-European V10		+2 laps

Retirements	Nat	Car	Laps	Reason
Enrique Bernoldi	BR	Arrows A22-Asiatech V10	46	crankshaft sensor
Alex Yoong	MAL	Minardi PS01-European V10	44	spin
Heinz-Harald Frentzen	D	Prost AP04-Acer V10	28	transmission
Jos Verstappen	NL	Arrows A22-Asiatech V10	25	fuel pressure
Mika Hakkinen	FIN	McLaren MP4-16-Mercedes V10	19	gearbox
Eddie Irvine	GB	Jaguar R2-Ford Cosworth V10	14	engine
David Coulthard	GB	McLaren MP4-16-Mercedes V10	6	engine
Jenson Button	GB	Benetton B201-Renault V10	4	engine
Jarno Trulli	I	Jordan EJ11-Honda V10	0	accident

FASTEST LAP   R Schumacher 1m25.073s lap 39 (152.353mph / 245.140kmh)

DRIVERS' CHAMPIONSHIP

1	Michael Schumacher	107
2	David Coulthard	57
3	Rubens Barrichello	54
4	Ralf Schumacher	48
5	Juan Pablo Montoya	25
6	Mika Hakkinen	24
7	Jacques Villeneuve	12
8	Nick Heidfeld	11
9	Kimi Raikkonen	9
	Jarno Trulli	9
11	Giancarlo Fisichella	8
12	Heinz-Harald Frentzen	6
13	Olivier Panis	5
	Jean Alesi	5
15	Eddie Irvine	4
16	Pedro de la Rosa	3
17	Jenson Button	2
18	Jos Verstappen	1

CONSTRUCTORS' CHAMPIONSHIP

1	Ferrari	161
2	McLaren-Mercedes	81
3	Williams-BMW	73
4	Sauber-Petronas	20
5	BAR-Honda	17
6	Jordan-Honda	16
7	Benetton-Renault	10
8	Jaguar-Ford Cosworth	7
9	Prost-Acer	4
10	Arrows-Asiatech	1

SAP UNITED STATES GRAND PRIX

WHAT'S THAT STRANGE SOUND EMANATING FROM MIKA HAKKINEN'S HELMET? SOUNDS A BIT LIKE AN ALARM CLOCK GOING OFF. . .

STAR-SPANGLED MANNER: Hakkinen was mighty all weekend and proved he hadn't lost the knack of popping the bubbly, even though he was somewhat short of practice

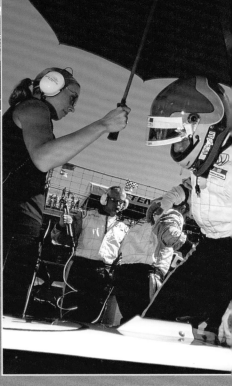

MIKA HAKKINEN WAS IN A RELAXED MOOD ALL WEEKEND
at Indianapolis – that much was obvious from the moment he set
foot in the paddock. At his world title-winning peak, the Finn
could be an awkward communicator, if only because he was
usually too wrapped up in other things to be worrying about banal
questions relating to team orders, brake balance or some such.

At Indianapolis, however, he was bubbling like a 15-year-old
contemplating a first date. He was pumped up, dryly amusing –
and outrageously fast. His pace-setting lap on Friday was no big
deal. As McLaren is usually at pains to point out (normally when
its cars are about seventh and ninth on the opening day of a
meeting), free practice results don't tell you a great deal. But
irrespective of his fuel load, you could see from the way he danced
over the kerbs that Hakkinen was committed as rarely before this
season. It was the same story in qualifying, too: yes, Michael
Schumacher beat him to pole by a couple of tenths, but McLaren's
greatest strength in 2001 was its race pace. For Mika to be that
close was a good omen.

**MICHAEL SCHUMACHER BEAT HIM TO POLE BY A COUPLE
OF TENTHS, BUT McLAREN'S GREATEST STRENGTH IN
2001 WAS ITS RACE PACE. FOR MIKA TO BE THAT CLOSE
WAS A GOOD OMEN**

CHASE THE ACE: Montoya
begins to exert pressure
on Schuey (below).
Above, from left:
Heidfeld did another
top job; Jordan's crew
wrestles an escaped
anaconda in the pits
(possibly); Villeneuve
gets ready to have a
crap day; Irvine got the
better of de la Rosa for
the first time in eons

SHOW OF FAITH

Except that he didn't start second. Nothing to do with McLaren's occasionally defective launch control this time, but the consequence of an incident during the pre-race warm-up (or rather one of two incidents, because he crashed quite heavily late in the session).

After sitting in a queue of cars waiting to exit the pits, Hakkinen mistakenly jumped a red light. That he had broken the rules was beyond doubt, but he had not done so intentionally and, as he pointed out quite reasonably, he had been unsighted. A fine or a slap on the wrist would have done – Mika is no dunce when it comes to track etiquette – but instead the stewards opted to give him a retrospective penalty and discount his best qualifying time, as a result of which he slipped to fourth on the grid. And you thought he was fired up during the first two days. . .

His race pace wasn't immediately manifest and in the early stages he lay fifth, behind Rubens Barrichello (who forged his way to the front on a light fuel load), Schuey and the Williams-BMWs of Juan Pablo Montoya and Ralf Schumacher.

Of the leading quartet, Montoya initially looked to be in the best shape. His Michelins took time to reach peak efficiency, but once they had, he slipped ahead of Schuey and breezed into the lead when Barrichello made his first scheduled stop.

Montoya suffered a hydraulic failure not long after rejoining, however, by which stage Hakkinen – running a long, 45-lap stint – had progressed to the front of the field as his rivals peeled in for fresh fuel and tyres. Quick, consistent and requiring a less time-consuming top-up, Hakkinen was still ahead after finally making

Formula One is by nature an extravagant sport. It struck some people as a little tasteless that the whole, opulent show should be taken to the United States little more than two weeks after appalling terrorist attacks in New York and Washington.

There was a fine line to be trodden but FIA president Max Mosley was quite clear on the subject. "We should never concede to terrorism," he said. Absolutely the right message, of course, but there were still some people who felt uncomfortable that the race was taking place.

In the event it was unquestionably the right thing to have done. America used Indianapolis's second world championship grand prix as a showpiece that highlighted the way life was beginning to return to normal in the States.

Event sponsor SAP made a sizeable donation to a relief fund for attack victims and a charity collection was organised on Sunday morning – the first time such a thing had ever taken place at the Indianapolis Motor Speedway.

An enormous crowd turned up on raceday and most of them made full and enthusiastic use of small American flags that were handed out at the circuit entrance.

Michael Schumacher said: "We had to face reality and life goes on. It was great to see the faces of the American people and for us to go there and give them some enjoyment."

Jarno Trulli (above), meanwhile, sent one of his crash helmets to New York mayor Rudolph Giuliani, so that it could be auctioned for charity. "I wanted to show that we are aware people are suffering," he said.

There was no great fanfare about proceedings, no mawkish sentiment, just quiet, reflective and appropriate dignity.

JENSON HEALER: Button leads Fisichella; the Brit's form improved late in the year

EDDIE IRVINE DROVE HIS BEST RACE SINCE CLAIMING, IN MID-SUMMER, THAT HE WAS THE SECOND BEST DRIVER IN F1

his stop. He might still have been in front even if Montoya had lasted; it would certainly have been close between them.

Hakkinen duly reeled off the remaining laps without undue alarm. With Schuey Snr acting as rear gunner, Barrichello was on course to finish second and boost his chances of being runner-up in the world title chase. Was. His engine had been losing oil pressure, however, and with two laps to go it blew, so the world champion inherited second.

Despite running a lighter, two-stop fuel load, Schuey Jnr had spent the first part of the race stuck behind the more heavily laden Montoya and he later spun off. David Coulthard thus took third – the first time all season that both McLaren drivers had finished on the podium.

Jarno Trulli finished fourth on the road for Jordan-Honda, although in keeping with his run of bad luck he was turfed out because the underfloor skid plate had worn away by more than the permitted amount. After the end of the season, however, a court of appeal reinstated the Italian and the original result stood. Eddie Irvine was fifth after driving his finest race since claiming, in mid-summer, that he was the second best driver in F1. (In recent events he had merely been the second best driver at Jaguar.)

Nick Heidfeld, no stranger to the final couple of paragraphs in several chapters of this book, did his customarily sterling job to take sixth. His team-mate Kimi Raikkonen might have featured, too, had he not damaged his suspension when he biffed Trulli early on. ∎

INDIANA POLISH

You are walking along a path, minding your own business, when a portly, yellow-jacketed chap, possibly old enough to have officiated at the inaugural Indianapolis 500 in 1911, stops to ask: "May I help you, sir?"

That's fine in itself, but when it happens every 200 metres it becomes more than a minor hindrance. Call it polite inefficiency.

As befits the home of the Indy 500, America's most famous race, nothing is done on a small scale. From the grandstands to the burger stalls via the media room, it's an enormodrome with atmosphere to match.

It is perhaps ironic, however, that the F1 track – built within the confines of the famous, 2.5-mile oval – is tight and fiddly for the most part, although the final, banked turn and main straight (borrowed from said oval) represent the longest flat-out blast of the F1 season, at about 24 seconds.

If you want to make a real racing weekend of it, the area has other attractions, too. At grand prix time there was a sprint car race on Friday evening at the nearby Indiana State Fairgrounds, plus a NASCAR stock car event on Saturday night at Indianapolis Raceway Park.

America has been indifferent to F1 for many years – and during race weekend many US papers gave more space to their home-spun NASCAR heroes than they did to the F1 invaders. But the US cares about Indy: the event was better supported in 2001 than many had predicted it would be.

Running a grand prix here might be a cynical ploy to re-establish F1 in the States, but it could succeed in the long term.

ACCESS RATING FOR BRITS ✱✱✱
About three hours by car from Chicago. Proliferation of things to do – eg extra-curricular motor sport, jazz clubs, shopping (Timberland shoes are about £40 per pair cheaper than the UK) – make it worth the effort

STARTING GRID

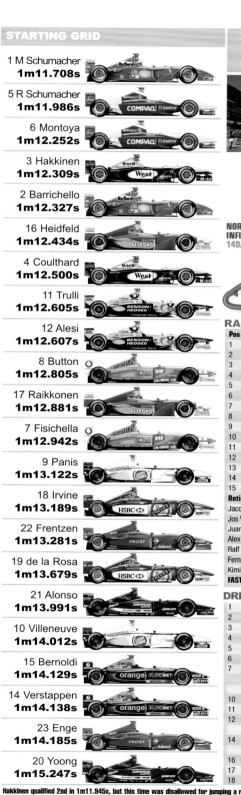

1 M Schumacher
1m11.708s

5 R Schumacher
1m11.986s

6 Montoya
1m12.252s

3 Hakkinen
1m12.309s

2 Barrichello
1m12.327s

16 Heidfeld
1m12.434s

4 Coulthard
1m12.500s

11 Trulli
1m12.605s

12 Alesi
1m12.607s

8 Button
1m12.805s

17 Raikkonen
1m12.881s

7 Fisichella
1m12.942s

9 Panis
1m13.122s

18 Irvine
1m13.189s

22 Frentzen
1m13.281s

19 de la Rosa
1m13.679s

21 Alonso
1m13.991s

10 Villeneuve
1m14.012s

15 Bernoldi
1m14.129s

14 Verstappen
1m14.138s

23 Enge
1m14.185s

20 Yoong
1m15.247s

September 30 2001
INDIANAPOLIS MOTOR SPEEDWAY, INDIANA
CIRCUIT LENGTH: 2.605miles / 4.192km

mph/kmh
❷ gear

RACE CLASSIFICATION

Pos	Driver	Nat	Car	Laps	Time
1	Mika Hakkinen	FIN	McLaren MP4-16-Mercedes V10	73	1h32m42.840s
2	Michael Schumacher	D	Ferrari F2001-Ferrari V10	73	+11.046s
3	David Coulthard	GB	McLaren MP4-16-Mercedes V10	73	+12.043s
4	Jarno Trulli	I	Jordan EJ11-Honda V10	73	+57.423s
5	Eddie Irvine	GB	Jaguar R2-Ford Cosworth V10	73	+1m12.434s
6	Nick Heidfeld	D	Sauber C20-Petronas V10	73	+1m12.996s
7	Jean Alesi	F	Jordan EJ11-Honda V10		+1 lap
8	Giancarlo Fisichella	I	Benetton B201-Renault V10		+1 lap
9	Jenson Button	GB	Benetton B201-Renault V10		+1 lap
10	Heinz-Harald Frentzen	D	Prost AP04-Acer V10		+1 lap
11	Olivier Panis	F	BAR 003-Honda V10		+1 lap
12	Pedro de la Rosa	E	Jaguar R2-Ford Cosworth V10		+1 lap
13	Enrique Bernoldi	BR	Arrows A22-Asiatech V10		+1 lap
14	Tomas Enge	CZ	Prost AP04-Acer V10		+1 lap
15	Rubens Barrichello	BR	Ferrari F2001-Ferrari V10		+2 laps

Retirements	Nat	Car	Laps	Reason
Jacques Villeneuve	CDN	BAR 003-Honda V10	45	accident
Jos Verstappen	NL	Arrows A22-Asiatech V10	44	engine
Juan Pablo Montoya	CO	Williams FW23-BMW V10	38	engine
Alex Yoong	MAL	Minardi PS01-European V10	38	gearbox
Ralf Schumacher	D	Williams FW23-BMW V10	36	spin
Fernando Alonso	E	Minardi PS01-European V10	36	driveshaft
Kimi Raikkonen	FIN	Sauber C20-Petronas V10	2	accident / driveshaft

FASTEST LAP   J P Montoya 1m14.448s lap 35 (125.957mph / 202.708kmh)

DRIVERS' CHAMPIONSHIP

1	Michael Schumacher	113
2	David Coulthard	61
3	Rubens Barrichello	54
4	Ralf Schumacher	48
5	Mika Hakkinen	34
6	Juan Pablo Montoya	25
7	Jacques Villeneuve	12
	Nick Heidfeld	12
	Jarno Trulli	12
10	Kimi Raikkonen	9
11	Giancarlo Fisichella	8
12	Eddie Irvine	6
	Heinz-Harald Frentzen	6
14	Olivier Panis	5
	Jean Alesi	5
16	Pedro de la Rosa	3
17	Jenson Button	2
18	Jos Verstappen	1

CONSTRUCTORS' CHAMPIONSHIP

1	Ferrari	167
2	McLaren-Mercedes	95
3	Williams-BMW	73
4	Sauber-Petronas	21
5	Jordan-Honda	19
6	BAR-Honda	17
7	Benetton-Renault	10
8	Jaguar-Ford Cosworth	9
9	Prost-Acer	4
10	Arrows-Asiatech	1

Hakkinen qualified 2nd in 1m11.945s, but this time was disallowed for jumping a red light during the warm-up

AND THERE *GOES* MURRAY

IT IS CUSTOMARY FOR *GRAND PRIX YEAR* TO ASK MURRAY WALKER TO DISCUSS A MAJOR F1 ISSUE, BUT NOT THIS TIME. IN THE TV LEGEND'S RETIREMENT YEAR, WE ARE GOING TO TALK ABOUT HIM

IT IS ABOUT HALF PAST FOUR IN the afternoon on Sunday September 30. A familiar face is poring over a raft of information bulletins in the Indianapolis media room. Murray Walker. Totally dedicated. Always has been.

About two hours earlier he had brought down the curtain on a 52-year broadcasting career. Fittingly, Murray's last scheduled race in the booth was won by Mika Hakkinen, another man about to take a break from the sport. During the weekend the Finn was asked what he thought about Walker's enduring

contribution to motor racing. "Great," he said, "and he can always come back, as I plan to do."

Murray's stint behind the microphone began in a wooden cabin at Silverstone in May 1949, when he had only a radio transmitter and a few flies for company. It ended at Indianapolis, where several hundred people gave him a rousing send-off at a surprise reception organised on Friday evening. Indianapolis Motor Speedway boss Tony George presented him with one of the 3.2 million original bricks that were used to pave the track in

WALKER!

What they were doing was wearing identical T-shirts sporting a simple message: "Thanks for the memories, Murray."

The subsequent party at 30,000 feet was quite a blast – it is apparently possible to get a champagne cork to fly the length of a 1-11 if your aim and angle are good – and the 78-year-old's retirement is unlikely to be any quieter. There's an autobiography to complete (the final research was done on a winter cruise), followed by an extensive promotional tour. For most of the 2002 F1 season, however, he will be a free agent.

"I don't quite know what I'm going to do," he says. "There has been no shortage

"MY TIME IN THE SPORT HAS BEEN AN UNALLOYED PLEASURE AND I DON'T WANT TO HANG AROUND LIKE A SPARE PART IN THE FUTURE"

1909. Varnished and mounted on a plinth, such things are usually the preserve of Indianapolis 500 winners. Murray was visibly touched and – for just about the first time in all the years most of us have known him – lost for words. Well, for a few seconds.

There was no such emotion after the race. "It hasn't really hit me yet that it's all over," he said. "It will probably be quite a few months before it sinks in."

Indy marked the second of two unexpected farewell bashes. European Minardi boss Paul Stoddart had a surprise in store after the Italian GP at Monza, where he had one of his European Aviation BAC 1-11s decorated during the weekend. "Murray usually flies with us," Stoddart said, "so while the 'plane was parked at Bergamo during the weekend we had a team of people flown in to relivery it with a tribute to Murray and to decorate the interior for a party on the return flight."

Walker was, again, rendered temporarily speechless.

"I was heading for the plane with Sue, Paul Stoddart's wife," he said, "when I saw all these people standing in a line leading to the steps. I wondered what on earth they were doing."

HIS MASTER'S CHOICE: Murray is bowing out for now (left), but might return to F1 in another role. A man at ease with his lot (above centre). In action at the Goodwood Revival Meeting (above). He is talking about buying himself a decent road 'bike as a retirement toy. Fact: Murray Walker is 78. . .

of offers, but I won't come along to the races just for the sake of being there. My time in the sport has been an unalloyed pleasure and I don't want to hang around like a spare part in the future. But if there is something worthwhile for me to do, I might still come along. I am in no hurry to commit to anything."

F1 boss Bernie Ecclestone made it clear that Murray will be welcomed back with open arms whenever he chooses. "I think he has done a brilliant job," he said, "and he can come to work for me. He can have a pass for life."

Team boss Eddie Jordan was one of many who paid tribute. "The thing I like about Murray," he said, "is that he has never had a bad word to say about anybody, and I respect him for that."

Equally, you'd be hard pressed to find anyone in the sport with a bad word to say about Murray.

GPY would like to extend its thanks to the owner of sports commentary's most vigorous vocal cords for his friendship and assistance over the years. You deserve a happy retirement. Enjoy it. ∎

PS: now that we've been nice to you, can we reserve you to do another foreword for us again next year? Thanks.

UJI TELEVISION JAPANESE GRAND PRIX

**SCHUEY PROMISED TO HELP
TEAM-MATE RUBENS BARRICHELLO'S
BID TO FINISH SECOND IN THE
WORLD TITLE RACE, BUT DRIVING
FASTER THAN A BULLET TRAIN
ON STEROIDS WASN'T EXACTLY
CO-OPERATIVE. IT DID BRING HIM
A 53RD F1 WIN, MIND**

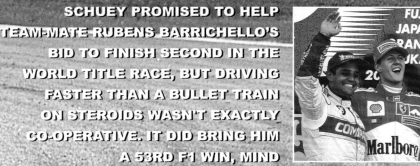

SCHUEY SHINE: the world champ heads for his 53rd career win (left), despite fierce attention from the man most likely to be his main menace in 2002. Above, Montoya and the winner pitch for toothpaste endorsement contracts while Coulthard struggles to raise more than a smirk

ON SUNDAY EVENING AFTER THE JAPANESE GRAND
Prix, hundreds of local fans remained patiently in the main
grandstand long after darkness had set in. Presently, a trio of men
clad in Ferrari racing apparel appeared from the tunnel that
connects the stand to the paddock.

It was just three mechanics wending their way home at the end
of a successful day, but the fans broke into a round of polite,
spontaneous applause. They recognised a job well done.

Michael Schumacher was the chief architect, of course, and his
53rd career victory was perhaps one of his best. It wasn't as
spectacular as some of his cameo performances in the wet, but it
was devastatingly effective. Prior to qualifying the Williams-
BMWs looked a good bet to set the pace, but Schuey had been
keeping his powder dry. Juan Pablo Montoya and Ralf
Schumacher were quick compared to everyone else – but big
brother was in a league of his own and totally untouchable.

It was the same story in the race. The BMW V10's extra grunt
allowed the Williams drivers to make better starts than the pole-
winner, but he had them both covered. Michelin's grooved tyres
work better if they are scrubbed in before the start. That makes
them more consistent – but in terms of outright speed they were
no match initially for Michael's fresh Bridgestones. The German
was 3.6 seconds clear after one lap, 6.3 after two and 8.2 after
three. He was pushing so hard that he made a couple of small
mistakes, but being Michael Schumacher he got away with them.
Montoya led the chase, but not until lap 10 did he manage to put
together a faster lap than the leader.

Schumacher's domination was never seriously challenged.

ONCE THE MICHELINS HIT THEIR PEAK THE WILLIAMS WAS MORE THAN A MATCH FOR FERRARI IN TERMS OF OUTRIGHT SPEED – BUT BY THEN MICHAEL WAS LONG GONE

Once the Michelins hit their peak the Williams was more than a
match for Ferrari in terms of outright speed – as proven by Ralf's
fastest lap – but by then Michael was long gone. The leader backed
off at the end and crossed the line 3.1 seconds to the good. As well
as increasing his historic tally of GP victories, he overtook Alain
Prost as the highest points-scorer in F1 history and equalled his
own record, shared with Nigel Mansell, for the most wins (nine) in
a season.

Montoya wasn't too impressed, however. "Michael's good," he
said, "but I don't think he'll ever match Ayrton Senna. If Ayrton had
lived he might have won another three or four championships. To
me he'll always be the best." Just what you need to help cement
what is already a prickly relationship...

David Coulthard inherited place for McLaren and thereby made
sure he secured second place behind Schuey in the points table –
the best performance of his career to date.

Ferrari sent Rubens Barrichello out with a light fuel load in
order to get him ahead of the Williams-BMWs. If the three-stop
strategy was effective, Michael was prepared to let Rubens
through to give the Brazilian a chance of finishing as runner-up in

BLOND FAREWELL:
Hakkinen indicates the
number of favours he
still owes David
Coulthard (above);
strop-and-go for Schuey
Jnr (top right); classified
as a finisher in the first
16 races of the year,
Alesi's record was
trashed (along with his
Jordan) when Raikkonen
provoked a violent shunt;
good news, Fisichella
made a fantastic start
and ran ahead of the
McLarens. . . bad news,
he spun on lap three

SPRY AND RETIRING

On the Wednesday prior to the Japanese Grand Prix, tyre supplier Bridgestone staged a press conference in Tokyo. Jean Alesi (above) was one of the drivers present – and he casually mentioned that he was going to retire from F1.

He knew that there would be no race deal for him at Jordan in 2002 – Japan's British F3 champion Takuma Sato had taken the seat alongside Giancarlo Fisichella – and he didn't fancy racing anywhere else.

The news came as something of a surprise, however. Even team boss Eddie Jordan wasn't aware of what Alesi was about to announce.

"I still adore driving and I love all the people I work with," he said, "but I accept there comes a time when you have to stop. As for the future, I am not ruling out anything – I'll wait and see what happens. Whatever I do, it will probably involve something with wheels."

As a result of his pronouncement, Alesi became something of a cause célèbre during the weekend. The Japanese fans have always had a soft spot for him and there were supportive banners all over the place even before he had made his intentions clear. When Jordan sent him out on low fuel and fresh tyres during Friday's free practice, he made full use of it and set the fastest time of the session. The crowd duly went bananas.

He bowed out with just one victory to his name – Canada, 1995 – but no regrets. Had he joined Williams rather than Ferrari in 1991, as he had the opportunity to, he might have had a world title or two to his name, but he's not bitter. "When I signed for Ferrari I thought the team was going to win the championship," he said. "It's a bit like the lottery. When you choose your numbers you always think they will win."

He crashed out of his final race – the only time in 2002 he failed to be classified as a finisher – but his commitment was absolute all weekend, just as it had been for his previous 200 grands prix.

LEAN AND MEAN: the top teams' 100 per cent reliability denied Button a point

RALF? HE OUGHT TO HAVE BEEN THIRD, BUT A STOP-GO PENALTY FOR CHICANE-CUTTING DROPPED HIM TO SIXTH. HE MADE ONE OR TWO OTHER SMALL ERRORS, TOO

the title chase. Although he dealt swiftly with Schuey Jnr, however, Barrichello found Montoya harder work. He lunged past at the chicane on lap two, but the Colombian responded with an equally bold move at the start of lap three and that was that. A momentary engine glitch during one stop also delayed Rubens, who slumped to fifth.

Mika Hakkinen was the quicker McLaren driver all weekend, but he backed off towards the end to gift Coulthard third place. "I wanted to pay him back for all the help he has given me in the past," Mika said with a blend of generosity and gross inaccuracy. Coulthard previously sacrificed at least two wins to Mika's cause, so the Finn stepped down from the sport (for now) with a sizeable debt still owing.

Ralf? He ought to have been third, but a stop-go penalty for chicane-cutting dropped him to sixth. He made one or two other small errors, too.

With the top three teams all getting both cars to the finish, there were no points available to anyone else. Giancarlo Fisichella starred for Benetton and ran fifth at the start, but he spun down the field on lap three. Although he recovered a handful of places, he later retired when he lost fourth gear. His team-mate Jenson Button was best of the rest, in seventh.

Sauber did enough to hold on to fourth place in the championship for constructors – the Swiss team's best-ever effort. It was some compensation for the fact that Nick Heidfeld (free practice) and Kimi Raikkonen (on lap six of the race) trashed one car apiece during the weekend. ■

EAST STERLING

Suzuka is a fantastic place, period. The track – which features F1's only Scalextric-style flyover – is peppered with quick corners and drivers relish it almost as much as they do Spa.

Its narrowness makes it perhaps even more of a challenge than the popular Belgian venue – although it also makes overtaking a trifle tough.

The atmosphere is refreshing, too. Motorsport is not quite as popular as it used to be in Japan, but at GP time Suzuka is packed solid. One route to the paddock takes you through an adjacent amusement park (where, on Thursday evening, Juan Pablo Montoya was still mucking about on rollercoasters long after most of his rivals had turned in). As you pick your way through the dense humanity, you can't help but absorb the locals' enthusiasm, which is as infectious as it is tangible. At some tracks it is hard to distinguish between enthusiasm and unruliness, but not here. The mood is genteel and it is a nice place to go racing, albeit a sod to get to if you live in Europe.

It also has a handy range of souvenir shops – and nowadays there aren't many places you can buy a quality plastic kit of Jody Scheckter's 1977 Wolf WR1 (winner that year in Argentina, Monaco and Canada). Not strictly a reason to make the trip, perhaps, but an added bonus all the same.

ACCESS RATING FOR BRITS **
Crap – but worth doing if you get the chance. A direct flight to Nagoya is the best bet, followed by train or cab. Going via Osaka is tolerable, but make sure you don't arrive too late for your connecting train (guess whose journey took 37 hours this season. . .)

STARTING GRID

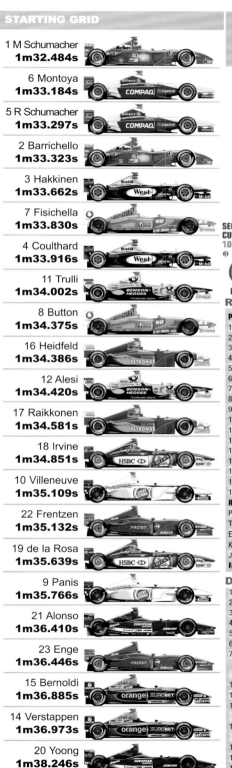

1 M Schumacher
1m32.484s

6 Montoya
1m33.184s

5 R Schumacher
1m33.297s

2 Barrichello
1m33.323s

3 Hakkinen
1m33.662s

7 Fisichella
1m33.830s

4 Coulthard
1m33.916s

11 Trulli
1m34.002s

8 Button
1m34.375s

16 Heidfeld
1m34.386s

12 Alesi
1m34.420s

17 Raikkonen
1m34.581s

18 Irvine
1m34.851s

10 Villeneuve
1m35.109s

22 Frentzen
1m35.132s

19 de la Rosa
1m35.639s

9 Panis
1m35.766s

21 Alonso
1m36.410s

23 Enge
1m36.446s

15 Bernoldi
1m36.885s

14 Verstappen
1m36.973s

20 Yoong
1m38.246s

October 14 2001
SUZUKA CIRCUIT INTERNATIONAL RACING COURSE,
INO-CHO, SUZUKA-CITY
CIRCUIT LENGTH: 3.641miles / 5.859km

mph/kmh
❷ gear

UNDERPASS

SPOON CURVE
100/161 ❸

DEGNER CURVE
130/209 ❼

HAIRPIN 45/72 ❻

DUNLOP CURVE

130 R
165/266 ❺

S CURVES
110/177 ❹

SECOND CURVE
100/161 ❸

CHICANE
45/72 ❶

FIRST CURVE 185/298 ❷

RACE CLASSIFICATION

Pos	Driver	Nat	Car	Laps	Time
1	Michael Schumacher	D	Ferrari F2001-Ferrari V10	53	1h27m33.298s
2	Juan Pablo Montoya	CO	Williams FW23-BMW V10	53	+3.154s
3	David Coulthard	GB	McLaren MP4-16-Mercedes V10	53	+23.262s
4	Mika Hakkinen	FIN	McLaren MP4-16-Mercedes V10	53	+35.539s
5	Rubens Barrichello	BR	Ferrari F2001-Ferrari V10	53	+36.544s
6	Ralf Schumacher	D	Williams FW23-BMW V10	53	+37.122s
7	Jenson Button	GB	Benetton B201-Renault V10	53	+1m37.102s
8	Jarno Trulli	I	Jordan EJ11-Honda V10		+1 lap
9	Nick Heidfeld	D	Sauber C20-Petronas V10		+1 lap
10	Jacques Villeneuve	CDN	BAR 003-Honda V10		+1 lap
11	Fernando Alonso	E	Minardi PS01-European V10		+1 lap
12	Heinz-Harald Frentzen	D	Prost AP04-Acer V10		+1 lap
13	Olivier Panis	F	BAR 003-Honda V10		+2 laps
14	Enrique Bernoldi	BR	Arrows A22-Asiatech V10		+2 laps
15	Jos Verstappen	NL	Arrows A22-Asiatech V10		+2 laps
16	Alex Yoong	MAL	Minardi PS01-European V10		+3 laps
17	Giancarlo Fisichella	I	Benetton B201-Renault V10		+6 laps

Retirements	Nat	Car	Laps	Reason
Pedro de la Rosa	E	Jaguar R2-Ford Cosworth V10	45	oil leak
Tomas Enge	CZ	Prost AP04-Acer V10	42	brakes
Eddie Irvine	GB	Jaguar R2-Ford Cosworth V10	24	out of fuel
Kimi Raikkonen	FIN	Sauber C20-Petronas V10	5	spin
Jean Alesi	F	Jordan EJ11-Honda V10	5	accident

FASTEST LAP R Schumacher lap 46 (135.194mph / 217.573km/h)

DRIVERS' CHAMPIONSHIP

1	Michael Schumacher	123
2	David Coulthard	65
3	Rubens Barrichello	56
4	Ralf Schumacher	49
5	Mika Hakkinen	37
6	Juan Pablo Montoya	31
7	Jacques Villeneuve	12
	Nick Heidfeld	12
	Jarno Trulli	12
10	Kimi Raikkonen	9
11	Giancarlo Fisichella	8
12	Eddie Irvine	6
	Heinz-Harald Frentzen	6
14	Olivier Panis	5
	Jean Alesi	5
16	Pedro de la Rosa	3
17	Jenson Button	2
18	Jos Verstappen	1

CONSTRUCTORS' CHAMPIONSHIP

1	Ferrari	179
2	McLaren-Mercedes	102
3	Williams-BMW	80
4	Sauber-Petronas	21
5	Jordan-Honda	19
6	BAR-Honda	17
7	Benetton-Renault	10
8	Jaguar-Ford Cosworth	9
9	Prost-Acer	4
10	Arrows-Asiatech	1

ALL THE WORLD'S A STAGE, BU

FORMULA ONE IS BECOMING MORE COMPETITIVE. IN 2000 FERRARI AND McLAREN BAGGED 322 POINTS TO THEIR RIVALS' 110. THIS TIME THE MARGIN WAS SLASHED BECAUSE WILLIAMS MADE IT A THREE-HORSE RACE (ALTHOUGH 281 V 161 STILL OUGHT TO MAKE THE REST WINCE)

REAR WING COMMANDER: ever wondered what 21 drivers spent most of the season looking at? We'll give you a clue (above), it wasn't the grid girls

IT MIGHT SOUND CHURLISH TO suggest Michael Schumacher had no serious opposition in 2001, but the facts bear it out.

The German collected 11 pole positions and nine wins en route to his fourth Formula One world title. No other driver took more than three of either. End of story.

But there is more than just Schumacher's abundant natural talent behind Ferrari's most successful period since the mid-Seventies. The Italian team is beautifully balanced and functions as a unit like no other, not least because the key players have been together so long. And technical director Ross Brawn's attention to detail is second to none.

The Prancing Horse's success the previous season did not lead the team to sit on its laurels. While McLaren relied on an improved version of Mercedes-Benz's

previous V10, Ferrari went for an all-new powerplant and that paid dividends. The McLarens were usually quick enough in race trim, but less frequently so in qualifying.

For a few weeks it looked as though David Coulthard might stop Schuey in his wheeltracks, but Monaco was a symbolic turning point. The Scot's pole position lap was one of the best by any driver all year: to outgun Schuey all around the streets of Monte Carlo takes some doing, and DC's margin of superiority was substantial. And then the car died on the grid. The fat lady wasn't singing, but she was certainly limbering up – and by the time teams peeled away from Silverstone in July she was pretty much in full voice.

Williams and BMW might have beaten McLaren to second in the championship for constructors but for reliability problems of their own. BMW's latest V10 was the

IOST WERE MERELY PLAYERS

JUST LIKE McLAREN, WILLIAMS MIGHT HAVE WON MORE THAN THE FOUR RACES THAT CAME ITS WAY

most powerful on the track, but was also among the most likely to detonate. Just like McLaren, Williams might have won more than the four races that came its way. Newcomer Juan Pablo Montoya was expected to shake up the establishment – and did, eventually. It took him a couple of races to settle, but he led his third GP and from France onwards was regularly faster in race trim than team-mate Ralf Schumacher.

It is just possible that F1 is on the verge of a golden era. Montoya's star credentials are obvious. Both the Schumachers are going to be around for a while, Coulthard and new McLaren signing Kimi Raikkonen will be potential race winners, Nick Heidfeld blossomed in 2001, Giancarlo Fisichella is driving better than ever, Jenson Button cannot be written off on the back of one indifferent season and Fernando Alonso looks a real gem. Sauber (with Felipe Massa) and Jordan (Takuma Sato) have also pledged their short-term faith in youth.

There is no shortage of talented drivers – but we could perhaps do with a few more competitive cars to accommodate them.

THE SPY WHO SLAGGED ME: Schuey and DC didn't bicker as much as usual, but did engage in some spontaneous espionage (top). Rare shot (above) – you usually have to use computer trickery to get Rubens in the same frame as Michael

OUR TOP 10 DRIVERS
(2000 RATINGS IN BRACKETS)
1 (1) MICHAEL SCHUMACHER
Bleedin' obvious, but the only option
2 (-) JUAN PABLO MONTOYA
Passed Schuey three times on track; compliment was never returned
3 (-) GIANCARLO FISICHELLA
Made Jenson Button look ordinary, which he isn't
4 (4) DAVID COULTHARD
Brazil, Austria, the Monaco pole lap. . . some of his finest moments
5 (7) RALF SCHUMACHER
Brilliant in the first half of the season. Unfortunately, the rules stipulate that there are 17 events
6 (-) NICK HEIDFELD
Fast. Dependable. Listens to Moby. Spearheaded Sauber's revival
7 (-) KIMI RAIKKONEN
Second year in car racing. Almost as fast as team-mate Heidfeld. Conan the Embryo
8 (-) FERNANDO ALONSO
Missed the Sex Pistols by four years. How can anyone be that young? Ready to win now, if he's given the right car
9 (2) MIKA HAKKINEN
Still as good as anyone on his day – but there weren't many of those in 2001
10 (-) JUSTIN WILSON
Most convincing FIA F3000 champ in the history of the world. Not strictly an F1 driver. Should be

BEST CARS
1 FERRARI F1-2001
No contest
2 WILLIAMS FW23
Went as well as it looked (below, left)
3 AUDI A4 AVANT TDI 130 QUATTRO
Pace, comfort, economy and much more reliable than a McLaren MP4-16

BEST PERFORMANCES*
1 MICHAEL SCHUMACHER, AUSTRALIA
Rolled car in practice, but went on to get pole and win with fastest lap
2 DAVID COULTHARD, BRAZIL

Conditions were ideal for Schuey.
DC outdrove him

3 GIANCARLO FISICHELLA, BELGIUM
Brilliance beyond scientific explanation
(far right)

4 JUAN PABLO MONTOYA, BRAZIL
Laid a marker Schuey won't forget

5 FERNANDO ALONSO, JAPAN
Embarrassed many better-heeled rivals

6 GRIMSBY TOWN
Against Liverpool in the Worthington Cup
(* at least, the best we can recall while
sitting in a Japanese hotel at the end of a
long weekend)

WORST PERFORMANCES

1 Jacques Villeneuve, United States
Has he finished yet?

2 Eddie Irvine (right), Silverstone-Monza
inclusive
"I'm the second-best driver in the world."
No you're not

3 England
Against Finland (away) and Greece (home)
at soccer, and against Australia at almost
everything (but especially cricket)

MOST DRUNKEN FANS
(2000 RATINGS IN BRACKETS)

1 (-) The Germans in Hungary

2 (5) The Finns in Hungary

3 (2) The Germans at Hockenheim

4 (3) The Germans at the Nürburgring

5 (6) The Germans in Belgium (right)

6 (-) The German on the tram platform
outside Albert Park, Melbourne, at about
midnight on Thursday before the race

BEST BATTLES

1 Juan Pablo Montoya v Michael
Schumacher, Brazil

2 David Coulthard v Ferrari, Austria (below)

3 Mika Hakkinen v Michael Schumacher,
Spain

MPWIJK F1
THE BOSS

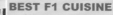

FLAT OUT!!

4 Jos 'The Boss' Verstappen (above, left)
v everybody, everywhere

5 Juan Pablo Montoya v Jacques Villeneuve
in the drivers' briefing room, Canada

6 Heinz-Harald Frentzen v Eddie Jordan,
(left) in the High Court

7 Schumacher brothers arguing about
startline etiquette, the Nürburgring

8 Juan Pablo Montoya v Michael Schumacher
in the drivers' briefing room, Japan

9 Journalists v Kimi Raikkonen, trying to
get more than three words out of him

10 Car park steward v Juan Pablo
Montoya, Indianapolis

YOU FAT BASTARD,
F1'S HEAVIEST DRIVERS

1 Rubens Barrichello 77kg

1 Olivier Panis 77kg

3 David Coulthard 75.5kg

4 Michael Schumacher 75kg

BLOODY LIGHTWEIGHTS

1 Nick Heidfeld 59kg

2 Jarno Trulli 60kg

3 Kimi Raikkonen 63kg (left)

4 Ricardo Zonta 64kg

WORST F1 CUISINE

1 Austria

2 Germany

3 Britain

4 Japan
(plus a special mention for Canada – icing
sugar and slices of orange don't belong on
bacon, so stop it)

BEST F1 CUISINE

1 Italy

2 Italy

3 Italian restaurants in countries other
than Italy